D0119465

Mrs Moneypenny Returns

columns from the Financial Times 2006 - 2008

MRS MONEYPENNY RETURNS

COLUMNS FROM THE FINANCIAL TIMES 2006 - 2008

Masterley Publishing

First published 2008 by
MASTERLEY PUBLISHING

Layout and Artwork: Suzette Field

ISBN: 978-0-9560654-0-7

Printed in the UK by CPI William Clowes Beccles NR34 7TL

This book is dedicated to Cost Centres 1, 2 and 3,
who are worth every penny.

Introduction

In October 2005 the *Weekend Financial Times* asked if I would like to rejoin its pages after an absence of more than three years. I declined. Mrs Moneypenny had been created for the *Weekend FT* magazine in October 1999 and had run every week until the magazine closed in July 2002. When the magazine was reinstated, I was not invited back.

The *FT* had managed well enough without me, I was being published elsewhere, and didn't see the need to add another weekly column to an already overburdened life. Running a business, writing, teaching and managing a family with three sons and a husband (none of whom knew how to operate the washing machine) was more than enough for me. But I thought it would be rude to turn the *FT* down flat, so I declined the invitation with a throwaway line that offered some hope. I would return, I said, when the Editor changed.

Six days later a new *FT* Editor was installed. Someone had obviously taken me seriously. I had no excuse, so in January 2006, Mrs Moneypenny returned to the pages of the *Weekend FT*.

This book is a selection of columns from my first two years back in the pages of a newspaper I have revered all my adult life. It is a privilege, and a pleasure, to write for it.

Family accounts

Jan 14, 2006

Three years and six months is a long time - 1,277 days can skip along very fast or crawl along very slowly, depending on how busy, interesting or fulfilling one's life is. For me, the 1,277 days since Mrs Moneypenny last appeared in the pages of the *Financial Times* seem to have sped by, no doubt helped by my insistence on raising three children at the same time as working full-time and pursuing a part-time academic career.

This column was launched in 1999 under slightly unusual circumstances. I had been approached by the *FT* to write a weekly piece on sex in the workplace. I declined, on the grounds that, although I then worked for a global bank headquartered in Europe that employed some 70,000 people, I had not (to the best of my knowledge) had sex with any of them. Further, as I explained at the time, I had never had sex in any of our workplaces - or indeed anyone else's. So I was woefully unqualified to be their columnist. Plus, I added for good measure, I was living in Japan, running a part of the bank that employed 220 people, 200 of whom were Japanese, had three children, the youngest of whom was under one, and was trying to finish my PhD, so I was a bit busy for sex. For some reason the *FT* thought that a real-life version of working motherhood would do instead.

But I did manage to write about sex, right from the start - the sex of my children. They are all boys, and I used to refer to them as sons numbers one, two and three. Some six years or so since I first penned this column, they have been renamed Cost Centres numbers one, two and three. They are now 16, 11 and seven, and have birthdays very close to each other, so if you do your maths you will realise that the other thing about sex in my life is that it only happens once a year, around Valentine's Day.

Personally, I do not believe rearing children to be a full-contact sport, and so Cost Centres numbers one and two are outsourced to boarding school; this, like all outsourcing, has both merits and drawbacks, but unlike, say, HSBC's back office operations, it is most certainly not a cost-saving measure. Indeed, I could not think of any other activity I might undertake (and this includes standing beside a lavatory and flushing £50 notes down it continually) that uses so much cash. But you work for a bank, I hear you cry! Surely you can afford a dozen children at boarding school! But I don't. In 2000 I left the bank and joined a small company in the West End of London that didn't even have a dishwasher. This might not have been a problem except that the kitchen was so small that I had to squeeze between the refrigerator and the sink to wash up - and I, as you will see from the illustration, tend more towards the Dawn French than the Kate Moss silhouette.

After a long battle I secured the dishwasher - a half-size one, but it was cheaper than the plastic surgery required to make me fit the gap next to the sink. That was five years ago, and since then much has changed. I led a management buyout of the company just over a year ago, and promptly moved us into a new office that not only has its own front door but a full-size dishwasher and a lot of room behind the sink.

The long-suffering (and Australian) Mr Moneypenny supplied the wine for the office-warming party, which tells you what he is doing these days - purveying wine to the chattering classes. This career development took place in mid-life, and at least beats a motorbike or a mistress, allegedly two of the interests many other middle-aged men adopt. Having spent 25 years in the television industry with great success, based on no prior qualifications other than having watched a lot of TV, Mr M's new career looks to be just as successful, given that he had no prior qualifications other than having drunk, in his lifetime, a lot of wine. Plus he is now even more useful as a corporate husband - not only can he still list the 23 left-handed batsmen to score a test century for Australia since the second world war, but he can tell you whether the Bordeaux you are thinking of choosing from the wine list is Left or Right bank and if it is from an appropriate vintage.

Not much else has changed, though - much to his disappointment and displeasure, he has failed to bring his golf handicap down to single figures. Maybe he might eventually manage to do so - given another 1,277 days.

Match point

Jan 21, 2006

It would take a brave person, I told Cost Centre No.1 the other day, to write a book on marriage. Mr M and I celebrated 17 years of survival at the end of 2005, and each year I am no less astonished that we have reached yet another anniversary.

Personally, I put this achievement down to Mr M's amazing patience with me, not least when I am standing in the middle of the kitchen admonishing all three Cost Centres, plus anyone else who dares venture in there, for their lack of appreciation of my good self. (Along the lines of, "Do you know how hard I work for you to have all these things; I never had your privileges at your age; are you aware of the opportunity cost of £7,500 per term?" and so on.)

My astonishment is not just that anyone could tolerate me for 17 years - and let's face it, I can hardly tolerate myself - but also, as I look around, I see all my girlfriends either extracting themselves from marriage, or choosing not to enter the institution in the first place.

Those new to my column (and indeed my life) should know that I have several aspirational girlfriends, so-called not because they aspire to anything in particular, but because all of them have at least one characteristic that I aspire to. My Most Glamorous Girlfriend, for a start, has recently been placed back on the secondary market by husband No. 2. Given how beautiful, educated, stylish and successful in her career MGG is, plus her ability to cook things out of cookbooks so that they turn out as they are illustrated, I do not expect her to be single for long. However, given that I provided the introduction to both her husbands, I am not volunteering my services as a dating agency a third time.

I have had more success, though, with my Single Girlfriend. SG, like Mr M an Australian, likes to play down the fact that early in her career she qualified as a chartered accountant. Unfashionably, I am quite keen on chartered accountants, and my only regret in life is that I never qualified as an ACA myself.

I was pressed into action when SG, after interviewing several candidates, including my Most Eligible Bachelor friend, took up with her personal trainer. I wouldn't want to be called a snob, but in my view personal trainers are fine for the purpose for which they are intended. They are not, in my opinion, prospective life partners.

I therefore introduced her to another ACA who, like her, long ago ceased to practise as such. In his case he has eschewed audit for corporate finance, and had also managed to eschew matrimony. He still has, because although SG has moved in with him and is due to have his child in April, she has declared herself not interested in getting married. Maybe after seeing how things have turned out for MGG after marrying two of my introductions, this might be a wise move.

I could carry on for pages: Most Telegenic Girlfriend, currently in the final legal stages of extraction; Other Single Girlfriend, continues to reject candidates after brief interviews and has instead bought substantial country house to share with dog; Wealthiest Girlfriend, heading towards 30 years of marriage (I need to get a few tips); Most Successful Girlfriend, has abandoned glittering career at world's most successful investment bank for position of full-time homemaker and mother of three cost centres under six, needs lobotomy but at least is still married. That's enough for now.

So what is a suitable gift after 17 years of marriage? After Mr

M and I had been up in a cable car to 4,000 metres to admire the view of Mont Blanc, he suggested a visit to the smart knitwear shop in Chamonix. I was sure that lack of oxygen caused him to offer to go clothes shopping with me, but on arrival my hopes were raised even further when he remarked that he had seen something particularly nice in the window. It was only when we got into the shop that I realised the garment he had espied was for him! I left the shop empty-handed.

Looking resplendent in his new sweater (like his other 17 sweaters, blue), Mr M, stricken with guilt, arranged to take me to a spa instead. At least, he got the brochure for the spa and gave it to me to book for myself, pleading lack of French, which for some bizarre reason is not compulsory for Australian schoolchildren. Marriage? As I said, it would take a brave person...

High table, low thoughts

Jan 28, 2006

The table centrepiece, for once, was not floral. It was a tall glass vase, a lighted candle within, engraved with the logo and date of the Bank of the Year awards, the function that I found myself at the other evening in the Great Room of the Grosvenor House hotel.

Admittedly some 1,600 people were present, so I was hardly alone, but I bet I was the only person to have cycled there in my evening wear from the office. Why cycle, my colleagues screamed at me, especially as I had just had Patrick the hairdresser attend our premises to try to make me marginally more presentable, and they could see all his good work coming undone in the rain that was threatening.

I cycled because I knew that when I left at the end of the evening, I didn't want to fight it out for a taxi with the other 1,599 (OK, 1,598, as I am sure that one guest, the Princess Royal, would have had a car waiting). And there was one person with whom I most certainly didn't want to fight for a taxi: someone at Bank of America who once dumped me when I didn't wish to be dumped.

As you know, I have been married for 17 years, so this event happened some 20-plus years' ago but I am one of those people who doesn't take well to being dumped. Having come face-to-face with the offending person at the drinks reception, I proffered my cheek gallantly and then marched straight across to the table plan to see where he was placed.

To my delight I discovered he was on table 87, which was so far away from the action as to be almost in another hotel, and certainly in a part of the room where people have to start off about three hours in advance if they wish to go to the loo. I, on the other hand, the dumpee, was sitting so close to the Princess Royal that I could have removed the diamante hairpin keeping her bun in place.

If I had reached over to adjust the Princess Royal's hair ornaments I would probably have been apprehended not only by her royal protection officer, seated discreetly nearby, but also Josef Ackermann, seated to her left, who runs Deutsche Bank. Deutsche were picking up all the big awards that night, including the ultimate prize of Bank of the Year, so they had wheeled out their big guns, and Dr Ackermann was not the only top executive present. Anshu Jain, their head of global markets, was sitting opposite him, and so I was finally able to observe him not only in the flesh but also at close quarters.

Anshu Jain is a legend in that goldfish bowl that is the world's capital markets. My dinner companions, at least two of whom had previously worked with this demigod (who has served time with both Merrill Lynch and Kidder Peabody), spoke of him in hushed and reverent terms. Now, I have long believed that Mr Jain is a great asset to the shareholders of Deutsche Bank, but what no one had ever bothered to tell me before was that he is quite young (about my age, I believe) and terribly handsome. So very handsome, I might add, that I am thinking of replacing the current picture I have over my desk (a Pearson share price chart - don't ask) with one of Mr Jain.

I didn't get as much time as I would have liked to gaze at Mr Jain, as I was busy running master classes in bow-tie assembly for the people at my own table. I was an honoured guest of the American bank whose logo is the emblem of a roaring stock market, but which seems seem incapable of hiring staff who can tie a bow-tie.

They kindly surrounded me with senior and distinguished bankers from their London office, including a lovely Spanish girl sheathed in red lace who works in their derivatives team. To my astonishment she turned out to have three children - I say astonishment because she really was so slim that I can only presume that she has to run around the shower to get wet. I am so envious of people who can have child after child and never lose their figure - I, on the other hand, only have to look at a sperm to put on 10kg.

Ten kilos is quite a weight, and the glass table centrepiece wasn't much lighter. I know this because I decided to take it with me at the end of the evening as a souvenir. This didn't seem inappropriate - I mean, given the etching of the date and event, it was hardly going to be used the following year. No-one batted an eyelid as I marched out of the Grosvenor House with a socking great vase (having extinguished the candle), unlocked my bicycle and set off into the wet night.

I displayed it in the hallway of our office the next day, and felt very proud of it until one of our staff pointed out that the apparent etching was nothing of the sort, but a peel-off sticker. So this is why they hadn't used flowers - it was the pinnacle of cheap corporate entertaining, the reusable table centrepiece. I feel terrible now that the sticker is off and we have a very nice plain vase - it feels more like stealing than souveniring. I promise I'll take it back - next year, if they ask me again. And as long as they don't seat me at table 87.

A well-husbanded resource

Mar 04, 2006

China, we are told, will be the next great economic superpower. It is a country that everyone in business has to take seriously and learn something about. Last weekend, the school attended by Cost Centre Number One held a conference about teaching Mandarin in schools and I discovered that by the time Cost Centre Number Two follows his brother to that school, Mandarin will be a compulsory subject for at least a year.

This reminded me of a letter once published in the *FT* about a column I used to write for the paper's previous Saturday magazine, *The Business*. The letter came from Benjamin James, then as now an employee of the law firm Bircham Dyson Bell and someone I have never met in my life. He mostly complained about the lack of men's fashion coverage in the *FT's How to Spend It* magazine, but also included a kind comment about my jottings. He went on to say that Mrs Moneypenny "is very popular in China, judging by the number of people asking to read her column when I was there last".

He was not to know that five years later, my Chinese readership would expand as never before. I have recently had a surprising number of e-mails from readers in China and had assumed they had been reading me on FT.com. Indeed, they have been accessing me online, but not in English. Unbeknown to me, the *FT* has been translating my column into Chinese and I am available to every one of the Chinese edition's registered users - more than 250,000 people.

The first I knew of this was when I received an e-mail from a Chinese reader asking me for the definition of "corporate husband". Apparently in the Chinese edition the *FT* had translated corporate husband into "economic husband".

I looked up the word "economic" on my favourite online dictionary. It has five different meanings, and the only one that could possibly apply to my husband is "having practical or industrial significance or uses: affecting material resources".

Let me assure you, all my readers in China and elsewhere, that Mr M certainly fits this definition. He has many practical uses and he also affects material resources. Practical uses include changing light bulbs and getting rid of spiders, although he's not tremendously handy with a power drill and flatly refuses to assemble anything resembling Ikea furniture.

He also affects material resources in both a positive way

(he earns a good salary and gets 40 per cent off our household wine through his wine business) and a negative one. True, he doesn't cost much to run in the way of food but his golf club membership is not cheap, and he also belongs to the Marylebone Cricket Club (a posh club, where he is a playing member) and has aspirant tastes when it comes to restaurants. Plus he is Australian and feels the need to visit regularly. Then there is the need to accumulate golf clubs made out of material that would do a space shuttle proud. And the now 18 blue sweaters, monthly golf magazines, 600-plus books on cricket, the endless number of ready-made supermarket curries and so on.

A corporate husband, for my readers in China, is a husband who is very supportive of his wife's business. Mr M accompanies me to client dinners and is excellent company; he takes particular care to engage the client's spouse in conversation and make them feel appreciated. He has also been known to play golf with my clients, give up his weekend to stay at their houses and find and deliver fabulous bottles of wine to them when I wish to send them a special present. What more could a girl ask for?

I am delighted to be appearing in the Chinese language edition of the *FT*, but it did come as a bit of a shock. I immediately e-mailed the man who runs the *FT* in Asia and suggested that he might have given me some warning. Of course, it is true to say that I (and any other warm-blooded heterosexual woman on the planet) would forgive this man anything. He has film-star looks (although is probably a bit thin for my liking) and, as far as I am concerned, can translate my column into any Asian language he wishes.

On reflection, perhaps I should have realised I was going to be translated into Chinese. The trials and tribulations of being a woman who works full time, with a husband and a home to manage and who is engaged in putting children through a hideously expensive education, are not restricted to the UK. Or even China.

The bicycle peeves

Mar 11, 2006

London is not always a safe city. I returned to the office the other day and noticed that my bicycle was not in its usual spot, tethered to the signpost outside the front door. I immediately assumed that it had been stolen.

Quite why anyone would wish to steal my bicycle I have no idea. It is eight years old, a relic from my time in Japan, when I cycled cost centre number two to school before going to work and so have a basket on the front and a child seat on the back. It also has a Japanese police tag, which is required by law there, but is useless here.

The last time it disappeared was from outside the Royal Automobile Club, when police removed it as a threat to the security of Her Majesty's Golden Jubilee procession down Pall Mall. They left no note and it was only thanks to the helpful suggestion of an RAC porter that I tracked it down to the Charing Cross pound and recovered it, after paying over a considerable amount of cash. I raged about this in print somewhere - who would consider my bicycle a security threat? - but was then reminded by a reader that Deutsche Bank had once lost a CEO to a bomb planted on a bicycle. (He was in an armoured Mercedes; the 20kg bomb in a school bag on a parked bike.)

Any mention of Deutsche Bank is enough to turn my thoughts towards Anshu Jain, the handsome and charming head of global markets whom I encountered (met is too strong a description) at the Bank of the Year awards in January. I am still in possession of the vase I took home as a souvenir of the occasion (between Thomson Financial, the sponsors, the Grosvenor House Hotel and the event-management company, I am not sure they know who owns it, so no one has asked me for it back), but without a picture of Mr Jain to put above my desk. After writing in this column that I wanted a picture of Mr Jain for my desk, I was cheered when the *FT* published a lengthy interview with him, together with sizeable picture. But it wasn't one I liked. I preferred the one they used above the masthead, but which was too small for me.

You may ask why I don't have pictures of cost centres numbers one, two and three, as other people might, or even one of Mr M. We work in an open-plan office, in dealing-desk-type configuration, and so space is at a premium, and anyway I don't need reminding of what they look like. It would be somewhat out of character, too, if I played the doting mother at the office, given that I am well known for outsourcing the first two costs centres to boarding school. This week I managed to outsource cost centre number three as well, to Val d'Isere on a ski trip. Half-term skiing in Val d'Isere as a family seems to me to be even more expensive than boarding school, so we don't do it. However, when another family asked if they could take number three with them, I jumped at the chance.

I booked his flight on Air Miles and realised we were in another league when I was contacted by the secretary of the father of the host family and told to upgrade him to business class. If this was not enough of a message, then when I did finally get round to calling them to ask how he was, I made the mistake of asking if he was going off happily to ski school each day. It turned out he was not going to ski school. A private tutor had been engaged to teach him and their child, also aged seven. They met up with the parents (also coached privately) for lunch. In retrospect, I am surprised they even flew commercial.

My business may be successful, but our family are not yet in the league of flying business class to Geneva for family holidays and having all-day private ski tuition. I am also not in the league of being able to buy a new bicycle every five minutes or even every seven years.

I had my PA call the local council and even the police in an effort to find out who might have taken my bicycle. The guilty party had even, I pointed out, taken the hefty lock (which they would have to have hacksawed through).

I think it was at this point that my PA asked me when I had last used my bike. I couldn't recall exactly, so I flicked back through the diary and remembered that I had cycled to Bond

Street tube station to catch the train to Canary Wharf a few days earlier.

And then I remembered. I hadn't come back to Bond Street that day, but had met someone in the Strand for lunch instead. Which in turn meant that my bike had not been stolen, but was safely attached to a lamppost near Bond Street tube. From which I recovered it the next morning. Maybe London is a safer city than I thought.

Hot dates

Apr 01, 2006

I am going to give up writing this column. This week will be the last one. You would be forgiven for thinking that I had already stopped. Two weeks ago my *FT* e-mail stopped working, and readers writing in were told "this user does not exist". This was especially unfortunate as I had written that weekend about Mr M's very attractive new golf teacher, for whom I am looking for a new boyfriend. She has promised me that she will have Mr M's handicap in single figures by the end of the summer provided a new boyfriend emerges. Early forties, former championship golfer, capable mother of two teenagers, interested in music - I thought male readers living west of London would have been writing in droves for her details.

The radio silence was not due to apathy, or even that all *FT* male readers over 40 who live west of London are happily married, but because my e-mail address had been accidentally disabled a few days before the column appeared. The problem has now been fixed and all e-mails will be duly forwarded to the lady in question.

Someone who shares Mr M's passion for cricket, if not for golf, is Bill Emmott, until this week the editor of *The Economist*. The current issue will carry his valedictory editorial comment, and I for one shall be eagerly opening my subscription copy. We first met after he wrote me a fan e-mail to the *FT* in 2000 when I was writing *Email from Tokyo*.

Emmott has no cost centres, which is presumably how he

can afford to give up full time employment on the young side (just) of 50. I am constantly criticised for using adjectives that verge on adulation, so I will choose some carefully to describe him: sanguine, witty, insightful. It helps that he was a Mrs Moneypenny fan before we met, and that we share a passion for all things Japanese. But the comparisons stop there. While his modesty means he will baulk at the description, in his position at *The Economist* he must have been one of the most influential men in the developed, and possibly the developing, world. Under his command it doubled its circulation to 1 million, among them some of the most important people in the world. Emmott, in print at least, is my favourite virtual Friday night date (usually in the bath). He has never worked anywhere but *The Economist*, so I am not sure how he will adapt to the outside world. I, on the other hand, am not sure how I will adapt to a Bill-free *Economist*, although I will continue to subscribe and can continue to read his views in his column for *Ushio*, a monthly owned by the Buddhist organisation Soka Gakkai.

I am somewhat amused that a proponent of the Iraq invasion such as Emmott writes a column on world affairs for Buddhists, but clearly there is a market, as a collection of the past two years' columns are promised in book form later this year. In the meantime you can read them on www.billemmott.com in both English and Japanese.

One thing I might miss is my invitation to *The Economist's* annual party, which is always held somewhere grand (Tate Britain, for example). There are always guests I'm interested to meet, and others with whom it is nice to catch up. A couple of years ago, one of those I caught up with was the former investment banker and serial company chairman, Sir Victor Blank. When I was 25 I advertised in *Private Eye* for a boyfriend. One applicant was the in-house legal counsel for a publicly quoted gaming company. He didn't last long, mainly because his idea of a good night out was a three-for-10 rights issue dinner. It did at least have the benefit of being at Charterhouse's dining rooms, and I did get to meet Victor Blank, then chairman and chief executive of the merchant bank.

That was in 1987, and we did not meet again until 2003 when Sir Victor was one of the select few to attend the 11 Downing Street charity launch of my book, Survival in the City. Now, in 2006, he has become the chairman of Lloyds TSB. Like Bill Emmott, Sir Victor has a passion for cricket and even has his own cricket pitch, something Mr M has long dreamed of. No doubt this accounts for his successful relationship with the former editor of The Mirror, Piers Morgan, also a keen cricket player and fan. Sir Victor was until recently the Trinity Mirror Group's chairman and at a charity breakfast the other day I asked Morgan, a man whose speeches are full of humour derived from criticism of others, what he thought of the Lloyds appointment. His public praise for Sir Victor was worth noting - he said he was one of the most supportive bosses he had ever worked for. I had found one of the few people for whom Morgan doesn't have a bad word.

The cricket season starts this month, (Lancashire v Hampshire at Old Trafford, April 18. Yes, it is April already. Look at the date of today's issue of the magazine. See you next week.

Pregnant pause

Apr 15, 2006

I am rather concerned. My secretary, the Lovely Lucinda, has developed a boyfriend. This is not the man from Credit Suisse with whom she went dancing until 6am, who (to use a metaphor from the capital markets) turned out to be rather better at origination than execution. No, we have a new candidate, who she has been interviewing for a while and has therefore, she has informed me, been promoted from candidate to boyfriend.

LL will be 34 this coming week and so she must be a prime candidate for marriage and children. With three people from our small company currently on maternity leave, I am very nervous about further pregnancies. With any luck some of them will have come back before the next wave leave. For two of the three away at the moment it is their first child, so presumably there will be more. The third person on maternity leave has just had their fifth child, all of them while working here, so if they all go in for five we will be able to expand the company considerably without ordering any new desks providing they get their timing right.

I must say that as a mother of three cost centres myself, I am all for women combining careers with children. As medical science has not yet delivered the mechanism for men to have children, it is going to have to be women, and it should not be a reason for them to give up their careers if they don't want to. What I do have trouble with is the idea, promulgated in some quarters, that women can have it all. As any working mother (or even non-working mother) can tell you, life is all about choices. You have to make the choice, not between career and family, but about the relative amount of time you can spend on each. Inevitably, if you choose to allocate more time to family than career, the career may not progress as fast as you might like.

One industry where women seem to be able to combine careers and multiple pregnancies effortlessly is asset management. Contrary to what the press might have you believe, Nicola Horlick is not the only female in the industry to have given birth six times. Helena Morrissey at Newton had her seventh last summer and Frances Davies, lately at Gartmore, has six. Katherine Garrett-Cox has four. I am not sure what it is about asset management that encouraged them to reproduce at such a rate, but maybe they have been heavily influenced by Lord Turner's pronouncements on pensions. I remember listening to a 45-minute presentation by Lord Turner and coming away remembering only one fact - that Albania was the only country in Europe with a birthrate that replenished the population. Perhaps, I thought at the time, they are short of television and contraceptives in Albania.

I discovered another working fund manager mother recently at, of all places, an awards ceremony in the US. The MC was Ali Velshi, an energetic and witty business presenter on CNN who arrived with a very attractive woman on his arm. I am used to television personalities turning up at events with eye candy, so assumed (how prejudiced can you be?) that she was some catwalk model that he had persuaded to accompany him for the evening, and I confess that on that basis I didn't rush to speak to her, although they were on my table. Of course this was a completely superficial judgment that I made on the worst possible grounds, and when I did eventually speak to her I realised I could not be more wrong. She was great company, very interesting and challenging to speak to, a single mother of two cost centres not dissimilar in age to two of mine, and a full-time fund manager to boot. Plus she has been accompanying Velshi to functions for two years, so this is hardly a fly-by-night romance. I liked her so much that we have remained in e-mail contact ever since, and on another trip across the pond more recently I had lunch with her at the Four Seasons.

I don't think I would care to be a female fund manager, cost centres or no, in the US these days. Not unless I wore trousers all the time - and that is not a metaphor, I literally would not like to have to wear a skirt. I never seem to pack enough tights when I go to the US, and on my first trip this year I ended up buying some there. Have you ever tried to buy a pair of tights (sorry, pantyhose) in the US without what they call a control-top? I will be the first to admit that my stomach could do with pulling in a bit, but in the US the control tops would give any normal size woman organ failure. Just getting them on uses up enough calories to render further exercise unnecessary. So the second time I packed my suspender belt and went to buy some stockings instead. Bloomingdale's vast hosiery department not only had no pantyhose without control tops, they had no stockings without elasticised tops - what they call "thigh-highs". These, I know from experience, cut off my circulation and fall down.

Back in England and in much more comfortable tights, I have moved my desk to next to the kitchen, to watch and see if any of the female staff are going off their breakfast. I am pleased to report that LL is eating as well as ever early in the morning. So far.

House rules

Apr 22, 2006

Cost centre #1 is doing his GCSEs this summer and will be 17 in October. I regard this as a major achievement - not for him, but for me. I deserve a pat on the back for having nurtured such a thriving child. I only wish I could do the same with houseplants.

My three cost centres are mercifully far apart in age. The first arrived when I was 27 years old, without a handbook, and it took me such a long time to find out how all the parts worked that I didn't go back to the showroom for five years. When you are expecting your first baby, you can avail yourself of an almost infinite number of books on the subject, on what to expect when you are expecting, what to expect in the first year and so on. I have not yet found the book that would really help when parenting a teenage child, one entitled *What to Expect When They Come Home with their First Love Bite*, probably.

Cost centre #1 attends a school in Berkshire that was founded in memory of the Iron Duke, the leader of the British forces that crushed those of Napoleon at the battle of Waterloo. Wellington went on to live to the ripe old age of 84 and when he died, there was a debate as to how to best honour him. At one stage it was planned for every town and city in the country to have their own statue, something that might have looked most incongruous in the 21st century. Fortunately sense prevailed and a school was built instead, the grounds donated by HM the Queen and the money coming from public subscription.

Incidentally, the government of the day awarded Wellington the handsome sum of £60,000 for dealing with Napoleon, and he magnanimously gave £40,000 of it back. Why, I wonder? Voluntary income tax? But it would be one way for the Chancellor to plug the hole in the public finances in 2006, though I can't see it catching on.

Wellington himself went to school in the shadow of Windsor Castle. Mr M subscribes to the Jeremy Clarkson view of this school - that it gives you five years of the best education money can buy, and then you spend the next 50 years living it down.

I have been seeing a bit of Windsor recently because cost centre #1 has had a run of girlfriends attending schools near there. He seems to be extraordinarily popular with their mothers, and so I am frequently visiting vast mansions with indoor swimming pools and Bentleys in the garage to deliver or collect him. As I mentioned, I have not yet found the perfect self-help book on parenting teenagers, and so have had to develop my own guidelines. He knows that there are many types of behaviour of which I disapprove, cigarettes and excessive alcohol being two of them. However, there is a sentence that I repeat constantly in the hope that he knows zero tolerance will be applied. I even text it to his telephone every time he goes out at night.

The other day, however, he was asked by the mother of a delightful girl at St George's, Ascot, who had invited him to stay, what his mother's house rules were. "No drugs and no unprotected sex," he replied, simply repeating my text message like a mantra.

It didn't get a great reaction, and I got a very icy stare when I collected him the next day. I have explained that it might have sounded as though we run a very permissive home. Which, sadly for him, we do not. Even if he is nearly 17.

Opera for beginners

Apr 29, 2006

Questions from children can be fiendishly difficult to answer. "Mummy, what is the point of opera if it doesn't make a profit?" was the latest one from cost centre #2 that stumped me. I coped much better with his brothers at the weekend. Cost centre #3: "Mummy, did the dinosaurs live before Jesus Christ?" Answer: Yes. Cost centre #1: "Please may I take a bottle of vodka back to school?" Answer: No.

Cost centre #2 (age 11) posed his killer question as we arrived at the Coliseum in London one evening recently. I had decided to devote some one-on-one parenting time to taking him to his first opera. Now, I am not a great opera fan, and have only been three times this century. In particular, I have not been a great fan of the English National Opera, as in the past they have expected you to understand the words for the absurd reason that they sing everything in English. I can't understand the words when some people speak in English, let alone manipulate the language by singing it in high octave voices.

But at last, sense has prevailed, and the ENO has installed a karaoke machine (OK, subtitles), which has made the whole experience more palatable, especially to 11-year-olds. The opera to which I took my son was the current production of *La Belle Helene*, an "Opera Bouffe" by Jacques Offenbach. Cost centre #2's follow-up question was to ask how Offenbach made a living if his work couldn't be staged without vast public subsidies and generous sponsors. I pointed out that as the first performance was in 1864, it was unlikely that he was still around to worry about such commercial niceties.

I confess to not having read any of the reviews before buying the tickets, so had no idea that the performance was going to be so entertaining, although I might have guessed had I had looked up a definition of "Opera Bouffe" - an opera in an extravagant burlesque style, with characters, music and other accompaniments to match. And I had also noticed that the translation had been done by Kit Hesketh Harvey, a very talented comic writer.

Mr Hesketh Harvey is half of Kit and the Widow, the celebrated duo who coincidentally played at the 30th birthday party of Lord G. Lord G is now quite a bit older and married to Lady G, who has been Mr M's golf partner in the recent winter mixed knock-out competition at our local club. Much to my amazement they won the competition! So Mr M's new and expensive (but still single) lady golf teacher must be having some effect.

I may not have known anything about *La Belle Helene* beforehand, but I could have predicted the plot - beautiful married woman has sex with someone to whom she is not married with dire consequences - because that is all I ever seem to see at the ENO. The last time was in 2002 to see *The Rape of*

Lucretia. This was Britten at his most sexist - women stay home sewing and flower arranging while men go off to war - and had some improbable casting. The man playing the Prince of Rome was so impossibly handsome that it was completely implausible that anyone, even Lucretia, would fight him off if he pitched up in their bedroom.

Dame Felicity Lott as Helen of Sparta was looking much more promising from the start. This is a woman who will be 59 on May 8, but is in astonishingly good nick and looked very sexy in a range of satin nightwear. Most women over 40 shouldn't wear bare arms, but apart from a few brief moments hers were on display throughout and made me think that I really should join a gym. The director even had her singing while bouncing on a bed, rolling over the floor as if in a school gym lesson, as well as standing on a pool lounger in a hat - pretty good multi- tasking. I wasn't so convinced by the concept of running off with Toby Spence, who played Paris. Not, you understand, that he is unattractive - far from it, and we saw a lot of his torso - more that the idea of taking a younger lover has never appealed to me. Mr Spence was born in 1969, 21 years after Dame Felicity. For me, that kind of age gap works better in the opposite direction.

I had very few criticisms of the evening, which cost centre #2 thoroughly enjoyed (although why does Laurent Pelly, the director, need quite so much hyperbole in his biographical notes and will someone please take new photographs for future programmes of ENO executive Loretta Tomasi and Jon Florsheim of ENO sponsor Sky?). However, it didn't help my attempts to develop an equal opportunity household when, having had her husband sent off to Crete, Helen then packed his case for him.

The curse of the BlackBerry meant that 10 minutes before curtain up I had been doing my e-mail and wasn't in a great mood. But the production was so entertaining and such a visual as well as musical treat that it was completely uplifting and the best kind of diversionary activity possible. Which is, after all, probably the point of opera. Even if it isn't profitable.

MATCH POINTLESS

May 06, 2006

The offer was one that I most definitely could refuse. In February this year I was invited to accompany Raymond Blanc, the chef- proprietor of Le Manoir aux Quat' Saisons, to watch Arsenal play Real Madrid, travelling on the players' plane.

My reason for refusing was not that the FT strongly discourages its contributors from accepting free flights. On the rare occasions when this is allowed, the policy requires contributors to state in the article that this is what they have done. So, I would like publicly to state that Arsenal offered me a free trip to Madrid. The reason I refused was this: I am not a fan of association football (soccer to those of you reading this in the international edition of the *FT*). I just cannot see the point of it. I have been to live football matches and know what it can sometimes involve: 45 minutes of no score, followed by another 45 minutes of no score, followed by 30 minutes of extra time with no score. At this point it often reverts to a penalty shoot-out, which is over in about 10 minutes. Why it is necessary to endure two hours of nothing happening before this I will never understand. The thought of going all the way to Spain to spend the evening potentially watching nothing happening sounded like far too much effort.

When I was first dating Mr M, he took me to several Australian rules football matches. These were very exciting, involving four periods of 25 minutes each when something was always happening and goals were always scored. This year is Mr M's 50th birthday, and it falls on the day of the Australian Rules Grand Final. Instead of a party, he has asked for a trip to the match. As the last time he attended the Grand Final his team won (admittedly this was on his 10th birthday), our attendance may bode well for them.

The reason for the offer of the visit to Madrid was that I had been inquiring about Diamond Club membership of Arsenal FC. I had heard that one of the ways the club was seeking to fund its new Emirates Stadium was to create an exclusive members' club with its own clubhouse and special seating. Nothing particularly new or exciting about this, but I had also heard that the cost of membership was no less than £100,000! Who on earth was paying this kind of money for the opportunity to watch a ball game that goes on for at least an hour and a half and may involve no scoring at all?

On further investigation it appears that the membership cost is a one-off £25,000, and the remainder of the money is for a season ticket for the first three seasons. Now, I may not know anything about football, but cost centre #3, age seven, supports Reading FC, who have just been promoted to the Premiership, and he has been pressing for a season ticket for next season, so I have been looking at prices. For him there will be change from £200 - and he will get to see Arsenal when they play Reading. Even for his father (as I assume one cannot send a seven-year-old to watch a football match unaccompanied, more's the pity) there will be change from £600. So £25,000 to join and then £25,000 a season?!

This actually buys two seats for the whole season in a special stand at what is, I am told, a perfect spot by the halfway line. The rooms behind will be a dedicated clubhouse and Raymond Blanc will be doing the catering. I suppose at least you know that you can take a guest each week and that you won't be sitting with any of the proletariat, as your neighbours will all have shelled out the same amount of money. You can also use the facilities all year and all week round, taking your mates over for dinner even when there isn't a match on.

Now, that sounded like an idea. Some good food and drink with friends in an impressive surrounding without the need to watch the 90 minutes - even I could see that membership would have some appeal. I asked if I could have a temporary Diamond Club membership to see what the experience was like. That would be a much more congenial idea than dragging myself all the way to Madrid to watch a game. (In the event, there was precisely one goal in that match, scored by Thierry Henry in the 46th minute - see what I mean?)

One issue with my temporary membership is that the new stadium (and the clubhouse) doesn't open until August. At the moment it is a building site, and I have never looked particularly fetching in a hard hat. So, instead, while I was still allowed to take some friends for dinner at a stadium without the need to watch any football, it had to be at Highbury, Arsenal's famous old ground that is being turned into a residential development.

I may not support Arsenal myself but I know a lot of people who do. One of them is the retiring headmaster of the prep school attended by cost centre #2, where CC#1 cut his teeth and, more to the point, where I am a governor. This is a school that has produced among others Douglas Jardine, Max Hastings, Will Young and even Bill Gammell. I owe this headmaster a big debt of gratitude and what better way to repay it than to give a dinner for him at the home of the club he has supported faithfully for 53 years, since he was about the same age as CC#3?

The dinner was a great success and was preceded by a tour of the club (including the changing room, which is smaller than my bedroom - how does Thierry Henry find room to tie his shoelaces?). I can now see the attractions of dining at a football club, and it appears I am not alone, as Arsenal tell me they have sold two- thirds of the Diamond Club memberships available.

The food was most definitely not that of Monsieur Blanc but then neither was I presented with a bill for thousands of pounds. And best of all, I didn't have to watch 90 minutes of football.

Bout time

May 13, 2006

Strenuous physical activity with men the first time I meet them is not a regular feature of my life. Especially after 17 years of marriage and three children. But last week I managed to achieve this twice in a period of 24 hours. And the second time, I even got Mr M to watch.

I hope you will not be disappointed to learn that in both cases it took place fully clothed. Since my disappearance from this newspaper in 2002 I have taken up two new and rather violent sports - shooting and boxing. Shooting I have mentioned before, and no doubt will again, but boxing is a subject I have yet to discuss since my return to the *FT*.

I didn't intend to start boxing, and certainly don't consider myself any Hilary Swank. What happened was that I made a foolish promise to take up a fitness programme when I finished my PhD. On the day I passed my viva in 2002 I was back in the gym, and after six months was bored rigid with working out on machines. Boredom, I am told, is the number one enemy of exercise. I then engaged the services of a personal trainer who worked out of a boxing gym at Holborn, and found that exercise in the ring was a lot more interesting - as well as being a very effective way to use calories and train muscles.

I have never been a great fan of exercise, as I couldn't really see the point. Whether I exercise or not, I still seem to resemble Roseanne Barr more than Madonna. What I am sold on, though, is how much better I feel from exercising - more optimistic, more energetic, needing less sleep - all of which are very useful when I am trying to run a business/family/ weekly newspaper column simultaneously. Plus I suspect I may have increased my chances of living long enough to fund the education of cost centres # 1, 2 and 3.

I am no longer training in Holborn - too far to cycle now that work is very busy - so I currently have a trainer who comes to the office twice a week. This can only be temporary as our expansion means that my improvised basement gym will soon give way to desks. So I was really, really excited when I discovered that a boxing gym was opening near my home. When I say near, I mean I can see it from my kitchen window!

Thus at 9am on the early May bank holiday I was climbing through the ropes, hands wrapped in bandages and tape, to thump the hell out of the pads held up to me by John Houston. Houston has been training white collar boxers in London, but comes from our parts and has converted a farmyard outbuilding to accommodate a ring and several heavy bags. I had such fun, and got such a good workout, that I shall be there regularly from now on. (Cost - for 30 minutes of intense physical activity

- £25).

Just over 24 hours later, I found myself climbing through the ropes again - this time while on board a ship sailing to Guernsey. There are not many ships with a full size boxing ring, in fact only one - the Freedom of the Seas, confirmed this week by *Guinness World Records* as the largest cruise ship in the world. Mr M and I were on board for 36 hours, along with a few hundred other people, as a guest of one of the Girlfriends, who has a very grown-up job with Royal Caribbean, the ship's owner. With 1,500 crew and the potential to carry 4,000 passengers, this was more a full-scale resort than a ship, and I confess I was not wildly enthusiastic about 40 hours aboard. This is not just because I was worried about having no BlackBerry access, but more that my enthusiasm for cruising has been up there with my enthusiasm for opera and association football - I can do it, but only if absolutely necessary and to make someone else happy.

My Cruising Girlfriend wanted to convince me that ships like the Freedom of the Seas are not just for the "newly wed, the over-fed and the nearly dead". Well, I am not exactly newly wed but with the hot-and-cold running food on board I might well have ended up over- fed, and after an hour with Irish boxing trainer Robert Tynan in the ring (cost: $83) I was certainly very nearly dead. The next day I had lots of hurting muscles, some in places I didn't even know existed. But it convinced me that boxing was still a fabulous way to engage in strenuous physical activity. Whether you have met the man before or not.

Life with Welly

Jun 03, 2006

It rains quite a lot in England. June is upon us and yet it hasn't stopped raining for long enough to mow the lawns at Moneypenny Towers. Mr M claims that he absolutely cannot get through another summer without a ride-on mower. Personally I believe that the current mower is perfectly adequate and complements his daily exercise routine with a weekly workout.

The daily routine is a walk of almost two miles before breakfast with the newest cost centre, who is (unlike all the other cost centres) a girl, although, as a black Labrador yet to see her first birthday, she is marginally more manageable than a daughter. We had resisted a dog for many years, but I decided that I cannot get through another shooting season without my own dog. Just as I dream of a rain-free summer, I dream of the day when she sits patiently beside me at the peg and then goes off to collect the multitude of birds I have brought down from the sky. Of course before we get to that day, either (a) I have to get more accurate or (b) I have to discover a strain of bird with a genetic heart defect that drops dead on hearing a loud bang. Plus she has to have a little more training!

The shooting season is usually when I reintroduce myself to my Wellington boots, but they have come in handy recently with all that rain. The other weekend I even wore them to a rock concert. Mr M and I attended a mini-version of Live 8. I should confess that when Live 8 itself was on last July, we were picnicking at a different event 60 miles outside London. A former boss of Mr M, watching Bob Geldof, Pink Floyd etc on TV 12,000 miles away, called our mobile and asked if we were in Hyde Park. "No, mate," said Mr M, looking round the car park at the various luxury marques assembled - "we're at the Henley regatta, where poverty is already history."

The rock concert we attended also featured a pretty impressive line-up, including several Pink Floyd members, Eric Clapton, Bryan Ferry and even Georgie Fame. It had been organised by Gary Brooker of Procol Harum who I didn't recognise until he sang "A Whiter Shade of Pale". Jeremy Clarkson took the stage at one point and said how wonderful it was to see such a stellar group of musicians band together in support of an oppressed minority. Except this time the oppressed minority were not the third world, but those of us who like to be free to hunt, shoot and fish - which, these days, includes a lot of rich rock stars and motoring journalists. Hence the beneficiary of the concert was the Countryside Alliance, the venue was Highclere Castle, and the weather was so cold and damp that half the audience was wearing Wellington boots and shooting jackets - and the women, expensively coloured hair.

They all appeared again, as did the rain, a few days later at the Chelsea Flower Show. Here I had to attend the gala preview without Mr M, but the downpour had the helpful side effect of driving almost everyone into the main marquee. So between 7.15pm and 9pm, before going on to a splendid dinner party, I did 1.75 laps of the indoor exhibits during which time I encountered one flower, 17 chairmen or CEOs of FTSE 100 companies, 14 corporate brokers, six fund managers, three prominent financial PR advisers and a former leader of Her Majesty's Opposition. Despite this assiduous networking, I still managed to miss some people that I had hoped to meet. Dennis Stevenson of HBOS, where were you? Did no one ask you? Do you not like flowers?

The flower I did get to see was a daffodil. Walkers Bulbs have had the good sense to create a new daffodil in *FT*-salmon pink, and even more sensibly (from a PR perspective) to name it after my Welsh Girlfriend, Ffion Hague. She was there in person as well as in flower, delighted to have a daffodil named after her and pleased to tell me that she has written about a third of her forthcoming book on the ladies in the life of Lloyd George. Apparently there were several of these (we shall know more when the book comes out next year) but none of them had a daffodil named after them.

Wellingtons were required again to attend a race meeting in Yorkshire a few days later. Guests of our auditors, I was going to use the occasion to complain about the fact that we never get the same audit senior two years running, and so have to re-educate them every year. But I almost didn't get to register my complaint, as Wetherby Racecourse nearly decided to cancel the meeting. Because it was so wet. As I said, it rains a lot in England.

WORTH HER WEIGHT

Jun 17, 2006

The Lovely Lucinda has gone on a diet. I know this because in her usual organised fashion she has typed out her list of permitted foodstuffs and pinned it above her desk in our office.

She claims to have put on 10lbs since developing a boyfriend, and I have four specific theories as to why she has put on the weight. One: she is so happy that she is eating more. Two: now that she has secured a boyfriend, she has instinctively stopped trying to stay thin in order to obtain one. Three: the weight gain is unconnected to the boyfriend but is related to the fact that she gave up smoking at almost the same time as he arrived. Four: there is not enough physical activity in the relationship to burn off the calories.

LL must have concerns about the last of these, for alongside her meal plan she has also timetabled a weekly exercise regime. On Monday nights this includes meditation, though quite how meditation is going to burn calories, I do not know. LL told me that meditation is good for eliminating stress, but I had to inform her that as long as she worked for me it would remain highly unlikely that she would ever be able to eradicate it. Not a day goes by when LL doesn't have to fish me out of some new calamity, diary clash, failure to remember key dates and so forth.

The latest episode was when I went to a business school to teach an MBA class and left my telephone behind. No matter, I thought, and sent LL an e-mail from my BlackBerry informing her that as I had no phone all contact would have to be by e-mail. Then I promptly left my BlackBerry in a cab.

This did not affect my class, who were closeted with me for two hours. They are an interesting bunch. MBA students are now far more plentiful than they were 15 years ago when I was one, but having paid handsomely for their course (in the case of my students, some £28,000) they are no less demanding than I was. And quite right too. There is nothing like having to pay for something yourself to focus your mind on whether it is any good.

The question really, though, is whether an MBA is worth paying all that money for. As one student put it, her colleagues think it will be a Master's degree in B****r All. There is some truth in this, in that the degree is not designed to teach any specific skill, other than how to be better at management.

Whether people with MBAs are better managers than people without is debatable. I have met plenty of good managers who do not have an MBA, or even an undergraduate degree. I found that 50 per cent of my own learning experience came from the other people in the class, rather than from the teachers, and the only useful practical skill I took away, and have used regularly ever since, was how to sack people.

If people expect to emerge from an MBA with a skill set that will instantly transform them into millionaires, then they are likely to be disappointed. An MBA is a general management qualification, a chance to look more widely than your own experience at how businesses are managed and at the management theories that have gained credence over the years. It is likely to improve your analytical skills, to make you a more rounded and better-read person, to considerably widen your knowledge base (mostly, as I said, from studying with people from other walks of life).

What is certain, though, is that with the proliferation of MBAs, where you studied is far more important than it used to be. And MBA graduates will have only themselves to blame if the value of their qualification goes down rather than up because their alma mater slips in the rankings. Graduate students, support your schools! If you want it to be a great brand on your CV, help to keep it one! Support it with your money, with your time, with your advocacy. Harvard Business School alumni understand this - everyone else, "get with the program", as they say over there.

LL does not have an MBA, but she does a very good job of managing me nonetheless. In order to manage my expectations, she has put her new regular engagement - a Friday lunchtime run - in the diary. I was thus surprised to find her still typing away 1.30pm last Friday.

What, I asked, had happened to the lunchtime run? She admitted that she and the boyfriend had imbibed rather excessive qualities of wine the night before, and so she didn't feel up to it. Hmm. Alcohol. A fifth theory, perhaps, for the 10lbs.

True blue

Jun 24, 2006

Do you know how many people in the UK are Catholics? Or what proportion of families in the UK are stepfamilies? No? Then you are in good company - Mr M isn't sure either. He needed to know, because he has recently done his "Life in the UK" test, a mandatory pre-requirement for long-term UK residents applying for British passports. Although Mr M has had "indefinite leave to remain" stamped in his (Australian) passport since 1993, he still has to queue up with assorted other foreigners every time he re-enters the UK. So he has finally decided to apply for a British passport.

At the start of the test he was made to sign some onerous piece of paper promising not to disclose the questions, so I cannot confirm whether they included either of the two in my opening paragraph. But the answers can be found in the book he has to read in order to do the test - Life in the United Kingdom: A Journey to Citizenship - available in most good bookshops.

Despite the World Cup match schedule being published months in advance, Mr M still managed to book himself in for this test on the very afternoon when Australia was playing Japan. Regular readers will know of my total lack of interest in association football, but Mr M follows all forms of sport and in particular anything involving his native country. So how he could manage such a colossal scheduling error, goodness only knows. In the event he was texting me frantically from the waiting room asking me to look up the score on the internet. Ten minutes after kick-off, I was able to inform him that the answer was 0-0. This did not surprise me at all, as in my experience most association football games seem to end in this score.

Mr M then disappeared into the examination room until half-time to sit his test. I wondered how many of the Australian World Cup squad would be likely to pass a "Life in the UK" test? More than you might think. I looked up the player details and only two of them play for football clubs in Australia. (More worryingly, I discovered that most of them weigh less than I do, but we won't go into that.) Of the remainder, two play in Switzerland, three in Italy, two in Holland, one in Germany, one in Sweden, and one in Spain. Plus 11 of them play in the UK, mostly in the Premiership.

By the time Mr M emerged from the test and was sent to the waiting room to await the result, it was half-time, and the score was 1-0 to Japan. This news, relayed by me via text message, caused great despondency. The assembled might of Australia could not score against the even lighter (average weight 74.04kg as opposed to Australia's 78.66 kg) players of Japan? It is enough to make anyone down-under think of becoming a British citizen.

I wasn't worried about Mr M's test result, even though his knowledge on human rights (a subject that takes up a lot of room in the book) is a bit sketchy. His definition of an infringement of his human rights is when he is prevented from playing golf seven days a week. The exam is, in any case, multiple choice, so requires a limited degree of literacy and offers at least a one in four chance of getting each question right.

You might have thought that, having lived in the UK since the beginning of 1989, with the interruption of a few years in Asia, Mr M wouldn't have needed to read the book. Sadly for him, the questions would not have been very relevant to life in the UK as seen from his perspective. For that to be the case, the test would have had to include questions such as: what proportion of children in the UK is educated privately? (Answer: I have no idea but it can't be that many as it is so heinously expensive.) What is the wavelength frequency of Radio 5 live? (For supplementary marks give both the FM and AM frequencies.)

Who is the English bowler to have taken the highest number of wickets in an Ashes series? Which former actress in Emmerdale is married to Harry Kewell and in which reality TV show did she more recently appear? Which three Australian World Cup squad players play for English clubs not currently in the premiership? (Answer, for those of you keen to play this at dinner parties, Luke Wilkshire, Bristol City; Stan Lazaridis, Birmingham City and Tony Popovic, Crystal Palace.)

The goal by Japan should never have been allowed, according to Cost Centre #3, age seven, who explained at some length that a foul had occurred. But it was allowed, and so even passing his test didn't put Mr M in a good mood and he drove back to work in deep gloom, the end of the game approaching. Then suddenly, in the last eight minutes, Australia scored three goals. Which must have been as statistically unlikely as the chances of Mr M knowing what proportion of people in the UK are Catholic (10 per cent) or what proportion of children live in stepfamilies (10 per cent).

Breaking up is never easy

Jul 01, 2006

It is never a day for celebration when two people who have previously chosen to co-parent go their separate ways, but I didn't expect to be this miserable. And I haven't just been abandoned by a co-parent once, but twice. Before you all start e-mailing me the telephone numbers of good divorce lawyers, let me reassure you that my principal co-parent, Mr M, has not left me. And neither has the nanny. No, it's much worse than that.

As regular readers know, Cost Centres #1 and #2 are outsourced to boarding school. CC#2 attends the prep school that CC#1 was at previously, and for the nine years that we have had a child at the school, it has had one headmaster. He leaves this summer. We have had almost a year's notice of this, so it should not have been such a wrench, but it is. When you send a child to a boarding school for boys aged 8 to 13 and only

120 pupils, you form a very close working relationship with the headmaster who becomes your co- parent. You make many decisions together, ranging from the very minor (whether they should continue guitar lessons) to the very major (which school should they go on to next).

CC#1 was a challenging child at prep school and I have looked back at his reports from then to illustrate this: "I have been disappointed by several entries on CC#1's page in the Conduct File which criticise him for being argumentative and refusing to take 'no' for an answer. There are definitely times when he struggles to play things by the book and then doesn't respond well when told he must come into line. Unfortunately his reluctance to let the matter rest doesn't endear him to staff. A more diplomatic approach might serve him better." Sounds like his mother.

Mind you, the headmaster was challenging to deal with as well. Towards the end of his time as a pupil there, CC#1 talked me into letting him take a mobile phone back to school, which is completely against the rules. CC#1 was, inevitably, discovered, and the headmaster, whose rage was palpable, unfortunately chose to express his views on my error to Mr M in front of many other parents. This is from the subsequent letter I wrote to the headmaster: "You know there is only one problem I have ever had with you in seven years, namely your way of allowing your anger and frustration with the stupidity of parents (for which you have much cause, not only on my own account) to express itself. I would ask that if, during the remaining three months that we all have responsibility for CC#1, there needs to be further words by you to us on the subject of discipline, then you try to have them in a somewhat calmer state and a less public place."

See? It's a two-way relationship and like many marriages, has had its ups and downs. But it's better than a marriage because you can communicate more honestly (and you don't have to have sex with them). I can't imagine writing letters to Mr M in the same vein. ("You know that there is only one problem that I have ever had with you in 17 years of marriage, namely your way of allowing your obsession with sport to express itself. I would ask that if, during the remainder of the marriage, you really must retune every radio to Radio 5 Live, you put them back to Radio 4 afterwards.")

In 2003 CC#1 went on to another, much larger, school, where for three years we have co-parented successfully with one man and seen CC#1 through early experiments with alcohol, and arguments about Latin, to someone who holds several positions of responsibility, is predicted to attain good exam grades and represents the school in several sports.

But even when he is behaving well, CC#1 will play a blinder, like this e-mail to his rugby master last November, written in an attempt to miss a fixture and go to a party instead. "Sir, Unfortunately I have not been able to go home for a long time, and my parents would like to see me before the end of term, they have made a request that I be picked up at lunch if this is at all possible. If this goes ahead, I am unfortunately going to not be able to play tomorrow. Yours sincerely, CC#1."

How anyone knowing me would have believed that, I do not know. After it was forwarded to me by the aforementioned housemaster, I called CC#1 and set off an Exocet down the telephone, pointing out how stupid he had been and demanding that he apologised to all concerned.

The apology, when it came, was not what I had expected. "Dear all, I am very sorry for my attempt at a con today to miss the game tomorrow. I feel extremely silly to have not thought of something slightly better than that. I appreciate greatly that I have not been fired from the team, and will play like a caffeine-fuelled hound against the opposition to nail them back into their try line."

So far so good - and two years to go. Except that we are only getting one year - this week we received notification that the housemaster is retiring from running a house. So I am being abandoned again. I'm not great at rejection, and I especially resent having to start all over again breaking in a new co-parent.

Called to account

Jul 08, 2006

Names are important. I work for (indeed own a lot of) a company whose name consists of two words - the two surnames of its original founders. They were women; they were (and are) both married; and the names they used then and now professionally, and which are engraved in brass outside our front door, are their maiden names.

Moneypenny is not my maiden name. (I can't recall ever being what anyone would describe as a maiden, come to that.) I took warmly to the name after meeting Mr M, and if he hadn't married me I suspect I would have changed my name by deed poll, so impressed was I with it. Rather catchy, don't you think? People have asked why I haven't changed the name of the company from two surnames of other people to Moneypenny Inc since acquiring a majority stake. Are they mad?

There are two good reasons for not ditching the name. The most compelling is this. When acquired, the company had two principal assets: one was some cash in the bank, the other was money owed to it by customers who had not yet paid. Apart from that there were a few second-hand desks, some rather clapped-out filing cabinets, a number of computers out of their warranty period and a little bit of intellectual property. Oh, and a small dishwasher. If you added all this up, it came to less than half what we paid for the company. In layman's terms that meant that the vast majority of the price paid for the business was for its name. Having paid all that money for something, why on earth would I wish to chuck it out?

The other, less quantifiable, reason is this. One of the original two founders of our business still works here, and it would be an enormous insult to scratch her name off the door and replace it with mine while she was still coming in through it each day. I would draw an analogy here with one of the Girlfriends, who is currently with Mr Right #3. She married and divorced #1 and #2. I asked her if she was going to marry #3 and take his name. Yes, she said. Why? Her current surname, she explained, belonged to #2, and she thought it was a bit rude to be married to someone while using the name of a previous husband.

I am in awe of the founding partner who still works here. She is more accomplished than me, better educated, more beautiful, has a better figure (the last is not difficult) and is capable of bringing a man to his knees at 100 yards with a single look. (I am only able to do this if he has misplaced his glasses.) I respect her views on everything and would never argue with her. This is why, when we both get invited to drinks at Buckingham Palace, and she has to be there earlier than me because she is more important, I don't argue when she takes the car I have booked and promises to send it back for me. It is also why, when she then calls to say the traffic is so bad that it can't return to pick me up, I get on the Tube without complaining. It is also why, when I had struggled across Green Park, I smile sweetly when she says I look a bit stressed.

In particular, it is why I didn't argue with her when she and I caught the train back to London after a performance of *Cosi fan tutte* at Glyndebourne. She had marvelled at the music, while I had been riveted by the sight of the chairman of Marks & Spencer in a particularly natty dinner jacket. Arriving at Lewes station at 10pm, we found the next train to London was at 10.40pm.

I didn't argue with her when she said we should get on the train to Brighton and change on to the fast train to London. Of course, there was no fast train to London from Brighton at that time of night, and indeed no train at all for half an hour, but you would not have found me complaining as we wandered around the streets near Brighton station looking for a coffee at 11pm in ball gowns. (Did you know the M&S at Brighton station doesn't close until 11pm? Maybe they were expecting the chairman to return home via Brighton as well.)

Our founding partners did not employ any of their children in our business, and I have no intention of allowing my cost centres to work here either. Not everyone agrees with this policy, though. A man I know who has run a successful business - which carries his name over the door - for 20 years, employs his middle child. While being entertained at his company's annual party at the Victoria & Albert museum the other night (it will be a while before we are big enough to hire the V&A, I can tell you), I met the son, who wore a badge bearing a different surname. He had apparently had to take a new one on entering the company, complete with matching e-mail address, in order to ensure that clients didn't think they were dealing with the owner himself. After 11 months, I'm surprised he isn't having an identity crisis. His brother had worked there before him, and he too had been required to assume a new name. So maybe if they change their names, I could allow the cost centres to work for me. Moneypenny may be a great name, but perhaps it's a bit too catchy, after all.

Spreading herself around

Jul 22, 2006

Content, it used to be said, is king, but these days distribution is more important. You can have the greatest product in the world, but if you don't work hard enough to get it into the hands of the consumer, it won't flourish. That's why newspapers have publishers and why our business has me; I work assiduously at reaching potential clients. However, my energy and enthusiasm for attending social gatherings can lead people to believe that: (a) I will attend any event, even the opening of an envelope (this is only partly true - it depends on the size and shape of the envelope), (b) I can't afford to eat and drink at my own expense (totally untrue. I wish I didn't eat and drink so much, whoever is paying for it), and (c) I never see my family. This is not true, but I admit that I rarely see my family Monday to Thursday, not least because two of my three cost centres are outsourced to boarding school. Friday to Sunday, however, is a different matter. It has to be a very special invitation for me to attend, and that happens fewer than half a dozen times a year.

I accept invitations that I think will benefit the business, where I might meet or renew an acquaintance with someone who might recommend us or even become a client themselves. This may seem rather mercenary, but I won't grow our business by staying in and watching all those shows I tape on SkyPlus.

The other day I found myself among 300 people drinking champagne and eating canapes at a party thrown by the owner of a long- established business that recently listed on Aim by reversing into another company.

It is a truth universally acknowledged that the standard of canapes at London parties has improved significantly in the past 10 years. This is just as well, because if I am staying overnight in London they will comprise my dinner. With canapes, too, the quality may be excellent, but distribution is key. This was proved at a party hosted by Tiffany, which was so well attended that I was in danger of malnutrition. I finally resorted to locating the kitchen door and positioning myself accordingly.

Similarly, at my quoted friend's party the tuna sashimi and quails eggs were brought out sparingly at first, but most of the guests left after an hour, leaving the kitchen with a mountain of food. As one of those still around when it finally appeared, I realised that not only was I not going to need dinner, I wasn't going to need to eat for a week.

Distribution being key, I try to get round as many people as possible at these events, which is tough even if they are badged. Peering at someone's chest to see if I should be speaking to them appears at best rude and at worst lecherous, so I was impressed when I was set upon by a fellow guest who announced that she had been trying to track me down all evening. She had dealt with our company in the past and wanted to introduce herself. How did she know I was going to be there? She had requested the acceptance list in advance. I can see the wisdom of this, but if you don't know the host extremely well it might appear even more rude than peering at people's chests. I can't see myself calling up the elegant and accomplished Barbara Kovacs, vice-president and managing director of Tiffany in the UK, and asking to see her guest list in advance.

My antennae are always alert to potential Girlfriend material, and this girl certainly had the energy and the attitude to qualify, so I gave her my card. Yet I couldn't get out of my mind that I had met her before, and had already judged her worthy of

Girlfriend status. As we chatted, she heard me refer to my children as cost centres, and immediately asked if I wrote this column. She told me that she and her husband read it each week and thought he'd love to meet me, so she went off to find him, but I didn't see her again that evening.

The next day I suddenly remembered where we had met before. In the dying months of 1980 I had a brief romantic liaison with a dashing Oxford undergraduate who dumped me for another whom he subsequently married. This had upset me at the time, not least because I had liked her too and had lost them both as friends in one fell swoop.

If it's hard to ask for a guest list in advance, that's nothing compared with calling someone and asking if her husband is one of your former lovers. But I did, and I was right. No wonder she hadn't brought him back to meet me. He'd rejected me 26 years ago, and clearly hadn't changed his mind. Her excuse was that he'd been distracted by someone else's cleavage. Mine, I confess, is not as impressive as it was at 18. When it comes to personal assets, too, content is important, but distribution is king.

Subtle as a blunderbuss

Aug 05, 2006

Heat and dust. No, not just the title of a Merchant-Ivory film, or indeed (the other way around) a quotation from Milton. More the current focus of my thoughts. As I write, we are experiencing yet another heatwave in London. The streets around the office are littered each day with cardboard boxes, which proclaim that they used to contain portable air conditioners. We don't have any such nonsense in our own, non-air-conditioned offices - do you know how many desk fans you can buy from John Lewis for the price of one portable air conditioner (which, as you have to open the window to vent them, are relatively ineffective anyway)?

The heat is affecting everything. It is even affecting my shooting, hence the dust. Did you know that clay pigeons are made of recycled coal dust (well, compressed chalk and charcoal, if you are being picky)? And that in temperatures around 100F, they melt - or at the very least, go squidgy? When stacked on top of each other in this heat they have a tendency to stick together, and so when you try to fire them they stay resolutely in the launcher. This was most inconvenient last weekend, as I stood around with my gun mounted, waiting for a clay pigeon that stubbornly refused to leave its nest.

You may ask why I am still shooting clay pigeons in mid-summer. The answer I would like to give is that I am practising for the grouse season, which starts on August 12. But the sad truth is that, so far, no one has invited me grouse shooting this coming season. Yes, you read correctly. Maybe I didn't make myself clear. So far, no one has invited me grouse shooting this coming season. I find this astonishing, as I am sure you do. After all, if you own or rent a grouse moor in Yorkshire, Lancashire, Cumbria or even Scotland, what more interesting guest could you invite than me? Businesswoman, academic, occasional journalist, middle-aged overweight mother-of-three - I would have thought I had all the qualities of an ideal guest to decorate your grouse butt. I am a safe shot, good company and can even use a knife and fork.

By the time you read this I shall have spent an even more gun- filled weekend at the annual Game Fair, this year held at Broadlands, in Hampshire. There will be guns of every sort, shape and size on display and I plan to have a look at a few side- by- sides, especially as so many of my readers in the US were shocked to find that I shoot with an over-and-under. It was even suggested by one reader that I attend the annual Vintagers event in Orvis Sandanona, Millbrook, N.Y. this autumn, billed as "the premier side-by-side shoot in the world". I understand that this is an experience not to be missed, peopled by, and I quote, "hedge-fund types and trust- fund hang-outs dressed in breeks and shooting anything that moves". Well, I am not expecting to bump into too many "hedge-fund types" at the Game Fair, but there might be a few "trust-fund hang-outs", no doubt several of which own or rent grouse moors (had I mentioned that, so far, no one has invited me grouse shooting this coming season?).

I have not visited Broadlands before, although I know it as the family home of Louis, the first Earl Mountbatten of Burma, who was mentor and friend to both Prince Philip and his eldest son, the Prince of Wales, until the IRA assassinated him in 1979. The Mountbattens were frequent guests on the Royal Yacht Britannia, which was launched the same year the Queen was crowned and was taken out of service in 1997 for old age (she was 44, the same age as me). The parsimonious Blair government then decided not to replace her. This act has deprived our head of state of her annual cruise around the Western Isles of Scotland with her family, and so I was not surprised to hear that this year, for her 80th birthday, she decided to splash out and charter the Hebridean Princess, a small cruise ship that spends most of the year in Scottish waters.

I must say, I wouldn't mind doing exactly the same, although I might not wait until my 80th birthday. For me, one of the main attractions of the Hebridean Princess is that it has its own clay traps and clay shooting competitions, staged on deck. I am not sure whether they get many "hedge-fund types" or "trust-fund hang-outs" on board, but after the royal charter, you never know. Let's hope, for the sake of the dust-filled clay pigeons, that the heat off the coast of Scotland doesn't get to 100F.

Her Majesty is, of course, a keen follower of country pursuits, and her estate in Scotland at Balmoral, to which she will repair following her cruise, is well stocked with game. Your Majesty, if you are reading the *FT* this weekend, might I be so bold as to mention that, so far, no one has invited me grouse shooting this coming season?

Maternal instinct

Aug 12, 2006

Different people aspire to different things. As I write this, my only aspiration is to leave Heathrow Airport. I have been sitting on BA 1446 to Edinburgh for over an hour and a half and it has yet to leave the tarmac.

I am only going to Scotland for the afternoon, although at this rate it will be the evening before I get there. I will return later in the month with Cost Centre #1, on our annual pilgrimage to the Edinburgh Fringe. Last year, we were accompanied by one of CC#1's best friends from school. This was not a burden so much as a privilege. As a parent, I aspire to having a child like this friend - straight As in all subjects, 1st XV rugby, 1st XI cricket and, just to cap it all, interested and knowledgeable on current affairs and immensely polite and helpful around the house. Plus sensible with money, gets out of bed on time and puts his laundry in the bin rather than on the floor. I almost feel like paying his parents for taking him away with us.

Is this a new business idea, perhaps, a way of turning cost centres into profit centres: raise immaculately behaved and delightful children and then rent them out to people who don't have any and need some to stand in at a social event?

In fact, you wouldn't even have to be childless; you could just leave yours at home and take theirs instead. Now I come to think of it, why stop at children? Mr M is very good company and excellent at engaging client spouses in conversation about sport or wine, depending on their sex. Perhaps I should start renting him out to recoup the cost of the annual golf membership.

As CC#1's friend is his parents' second such offspring (he has an equally accomplished and delightful older sister who is about to go to Oxford), we shall call him Profit Centre #2. PC#2 came with us to St Tropez this year where, among others, we had houseguests from the US who were not familiar with the British education system. CC#1 was trying to explain to them and me why he considered a girl he knew to be a little more intellectually challenged than him. "Mum," he said "she is doing Single Award Science."

A word of explanation. In the days of the dinosaurs, when I attended school, we did examinations called O-levels at 16, for which most of us studied and got separate passes in the three sciences - physics, chemistry and biology. These days, even at ridiculously overpriced educational establishments such as that attended by CC#1, most students (including him) cover two-thirds of the syllabus for each subject, take three watered-down exams and get 3x2/3, ie two, exam credits - Dual Award Science. PC#2, being a superstar, crammed in extra lessons and did all three sciences in full. What I had not realised until recently is that it is possible to study one-third of the syllabus and take three really watered down exams - the Single Award Science of the girl in question.

Our American houseguests listened to this intently. "Let me get this straight," the husband said. "PC#2 is doing Science, CC#1 is doing Science Lite, and the girlfriend is doing Science Lite Decaffeinated." Indeed.

CC#1 is on holiday again right now, in Portugal, where together with three school friends he has rented a flat for a week. Many people are shocked that we have let him go away unsupervised. My Newest Girlfriend, an Australian in the fund management industry, was even more shocked that the landlord had only asked for a £300 deposit. "Presumably no flat-screen TVs or glassware," was her comment.

NG works with both traditional, long-only fund managers and a few hedge-fund managers, who one imagines have a more glamorous time of it. What, I asked her, did she do if the long-only managers aspired to run hedge funds instead? Apparently she makes them run a dummy hedge fund for a year and sees how they get on. If they do well, then they are in with a chance. NG also applies this test of aspiration at home. Her household has recently acquired a puppy, a pet for her young daughter. The daughter had asked for the pet a year ago. The answer was yes, provided she ran a "dummy" pet for a year, reading up on pet care and writing a project for her mother on dogs.

CC#1 aspired to owning a dog for years and was always denied one. He was mightily put out when, last year, once his aspirations had moved on (to a video iPod), we acquired a black Labrador bitch, a cute little puppy, to train up as a gun dog. He was even more put out when she recently went into season for the first time. Despite the Science Lite syllabus covering the menstrual cycle and everything anyone could want to know about the lining of the womb, he refused to enter the kitchen to make toast until either (a) I issued him with a full chemical warfare suit or (b) I preceded him with a mop and disinfectant.

No such nonsense, I am sure, at the home of PC#2, where they also have a Labrador. I did ask PC#2 once rather wistfully (after having a heated discussion about something with CC#1, no doubt alcohol or money, or both) whether he ever argued about anything with his parents. Yes, came the reply. What? "Whether or not I should do Greek GCSE." Arguing about Greek GCSE. Wouldn't that be something to aspire to?

Strike a chord

Aug 19, 2006

I refused a date with Hector Berlioz the other night. I just couldn't see what we would have in common. For a start, I am alive, and he is not, having died in March 1869, some 93 years before I was born. Then there is the little matter of the vast quantity of music he has written, whereas I have yet to write a note.

I hate classical music, as I told my Scottish girlfriend when she was trying to tempt me with the possibility of an evening with Berlioz. ScotG cannot be titled SG, which we know stands for Single Girlfriend, and in any case ScotG is most definitely not single, having been married to a former boyfriend of mine for many years. They make them tough in Scotland - ScotG gave birth to her second child on her bathroom floor.

ScotG was outraged at my use of the word "hate". Quite right too. The word "hate" is banned in the Moneypenny household, as in "I hate vegetables". In my view hate is such a strong emotion that it is unlikely to be truly felt except in the most extreme circumstances, from which I exclude such events as the occasional carrot arriving on a plate. "Love" is also an overused word, again implying such a strong emotion that I doubt most people really know what they mean when they are saying it, and thus it has passed into the vernacular as a debased currency.

Moneypenny offspring are encouraged to find substitutes for both these words unless they really mean them, thus "I am not keen on broccoli" and "I really like my PSP".

But ScotG's outrage was not at the casual use of the verb to hate. No, it was because the statement "I hate classical music" is too all-embracing and is, she says, much like someone saying "I hate the City". Which part of the City? Stockbroking, insurance, foreign-exchange traders? Classical music, she pointed out, is too broad a church for one to be able to hate every single facet of it.

Berlioz himself experienced all emotions at the extreme. He really did love and hate. He was even supposed to have been so moved by reading Virgil as a child that he wept. (I remember weeping at Virgil as a child as well, but mainly because I became so frustrated at the length of time it took me to translate passages of The Aeneid.)

Berlioz fell in love with an Irish actress called Harriet and wrote such alarmingly passionate letters to her that she refused to see him. She refused, for a long time, to attend a performance of the Symphonie Fantastique, which was inspired by his unrequited love for her.

While this entire trauma was going on he managed to win a major musical prize, the Prix de Rome, but also become engaged to someone else called Camille Moke. While on some jolly to Rome as part of his prize, he got a letter from Camille's mother telling him that the engagement had been broken and she had married someone more solvent! He resolved to return immediately to Paris and kill all three of them.

Fortunately (for them) he only got as far as Nice before he calmed down and changed his mind. Berlioz returned to the pursuit of Harriet instead and finally got her to both a performance of the symphony and to the altar, but like all infatuations, the reality was much less attractive than the idea and so he eventually left her and moved in with his mistress.

I am told that many other composers of classical music are equally fascinating - J.S. Bach managed to father 20 children (confusingly most of them became composers with names such as J.C. Bach, C.P.E. Bach, W.F. Bach and J.C.F. Bach) and fought with his bosses for a pay rise. Borodin researched cholesterol in between writing his symphonies. And Shostakovich was a football referee in his spare time. Brahms earned a living of sorts playing the piano in brothels - he was paid in beer. As for Wagner, well aside from the debts, affairs and political arrest, he was posthumously a strong influence on Hitler.

However, none of this persuaded me that I should go to the Albert Hall and hear the Royal Scottish National Orchestra, talented though I am sure they are, play the Symphonie Fantastique. Showing some solidarity with Harriet, I refused point blank to attend. ScotG and I went out to breakfast on the day of the performance while she tried to change my mind. I was much more interested in the attractive 46-year-old man with the golden retriever on the next table reading the *FT* while consuming his coffee. As I pointed out to ScotG, just because I am on a diet doesn't mean I shouldn't look at the menu. (You may ask how I knew he was 46? He told me! It's not just composers who can be persistent.)

Walking back from our breakfast down the street where my office is located, I noticed a blue plaque on the wall of a building on the opposite side of the road. "Hector Berlioz stayed here in 1851," it says. It turns out he had been sent over by the French government to look at the musical instruments in the Great Exhibition and walked from here to Hyde Park every day. It's a nice street, and I walk from it to places all over London each day. I had never noticed the blue plaque before - but now I know what else I have in common with Hector Berlioz.

Inclusion zone

Aug 26, 2006

Cyril is not a name that sounds very contemporary to me. To be honest, I don't know anyone called Cyril. I had never even met anyone called Cyril until the other weekend when I attended a wedding which was taken by the Right Reverend Cyril Guy

Ashton, who when he isn't taking weddings in other people's churches is known as the Bishop of Doncaster.

To be accurate he is known as the Suffragan Bishop, Doncaster. I confess to having encountered the word suffragan even less than I have encountered people called Cyril, so I looked it up, and it appears to mean a deputy, and only applies to bishops; hence you can't have, for example, a Suffragan CEO.

In which case, why do you need the word bishop as well as the word suffragan? Surely we could have Cyril, Suffragan of Doncaster? And I am not sure I understand what distinguishes a deputy bishop from his boss, in Cyril's case the rather jolly-sounding Bishop Jack, Bishop of Sheffield. As a suffragan, I understand, Cyril has "administrative and episcopal responsibilities but no jurisdictional functions". I don't know what other functions he has but, on the basis of only one sampling he is pretty good at taking weddings.

His ability to put everyone, the happy couple included, at their ease, to make everyone feel included (even with quite a large congregation) and to inject humour into the proceedings without ever letting us forget that this was a serious occasion, were skills I thought would not be out of place in the leadership of a public company. (He did toy with accountancy at one point in his career, so he might have made a good finance director!)

If I were the Archbishop of Canterbury, who arguably is the CEO that the Queen has put in charge of the Church of England, I would put Cyril in charge of the department that is charged with raising church attendance. His particular brand of ministry strikes me as something that many people would relate to.

You can find out some interesting things about Cyril on the internet (including, by the way, the fact that he doesn't look at all old-fashioned and is interested in classic cars and motorbikes), even an e-mail address that may or may not still work. This last I found rather incongruous, even for someone who wrote their masters thesis on the theology of the Roman Catholic Church. What was any minister thinking of when they signed up with Virgin as an ISP?

Unexpected but intriguing encounters recently have not been restricted to meeting someone called Cyril. I found myself in a club near Paddington Station the other day attending a farewell party for friends of mine who are moving overseas. It is called the Frontline Club and was founded by someone I have never met, a man called Vaughan Smith, an ex-army officer who with two others had previously established a company of the same name to sell news footage from dangerous parts of the world.

Most famous in his world for masquerading as a British officer to get the only uncensored footage of the Gulf war, in 2003 Smith started the Frontline Club to support those journalists, cameramen and photographers throughout the world who risk their lives in the course of their work.

On one level, it's an intimate little club in a Paddington backwater with an award-winning restaurant that is open to the public. But that is as useful a description as merely telling you that Cyril Ashton is a Church of England minister. Walking up the stairs - past framed newspaper front pages from conflicts past and present, and photographs that were been brought to the world from some of the most dangerous battlegrounds of modern times - I was moved to stand and take a few minutes to think of those whose very nature causes them to take enormous personal risk in the interest of bringing back independent footage or photographs from these events. Several people who have been associated with either the company or the club in their brief history have already lost their lives.

I am not a "real" journalist, in the sense that this is not how I earn a living; and most of the journalists I encounter in my daily life are doing nothing more dangerous than risking a heart attack by reporting on some of the pay packages of our business leaders; but it is worth remembering that there is a whole other breed out there who you are unlikely to meet propping up the bars of the Square Mile.

I stood and gazed at the iconic (and Pulitzer-prize winning) photograph taken by Joe Rosenthal, who died on Sunday aged 94, of American troops raising the flag on Mount Suribachi during the battle of Iwo Jima in 1945. As I studied it a thought struck me: I have only seen that photograph in a frame once before - and that was in a meeting room in the City.

Sadly, the recent Israeli-Hizbollah conflict was a reminder that there continues to be plenty of opportunity for Frontline members, and those who share their values, to work in very dangerous circumstances. I can't help but think that if there were more people like Cyril, not only in the churches but also in the mosques and synagogues of the world, there might not be so much of that opportunity. A thought, perhaps, that is not very contemporary.

The course of true love

Sep 02, 2006

Men who read the *FT* tend to have a certain appeal. I suppose it suggests that they might be interested in the same things as I am, and should we ever have to spend any time together, we would have something to talk about. Mr M, unsurprisingly, is not a regular *FT* reader. His preferred newspaper-reading modus operandi is to start from the back rather than the front, and as doing this with the *FT* brings you face to face with Lex (one of my earliest loves about the paper and still, for my money, a must-read every day) rather than a detailed critique of the test match, he is unlikely to convert.

But there are parts of the weekend paper that he enjoys (Tim Yeo's golf column, for a start, and Jancis Robinson, unsurprisingly), and I was most encouraged when he took up reading *How to Spend It* and then announced that he had found the perfect place for us to go for a romantic weekend sans enfants.

We had found ourselves bereft of children for a weekend in August because by some miracle we had managed to outsource all three of them simultaneously. Cost centre #3 was on holiday for three weeks with his nanny and her parents in Barbados, keeping an eye on Tony Blair. CC#2 was on holiday in Spain with the family of a schoolfriend, and CC#1 had managed to persuade someone who works with me to let him house-sit her flat in London. I was not wildly enthusiastic about this arrangement and in an attempt to get her to think carefully showed her the letter we had received from the landlord of the apartment he had recently rented with friends in Portugal, which explained why the deposit would not be returned. Without reproducing it in full, I will divulge that it mentioned, among other things, ice-cream marks on the ceiling, beer stains on the walls and ash on the towels, as well as some banana on the rug. Notwithstanding all this she still gave him the keys.

Hence I found myself off to spend a weekend on Islay, a large island off the west coast of Scotland, which according to the *FT* had a magical links golf course. You can fly to Islay in 30 minutes from Glasgow, but no, this didn't appeal (would the airline lose the clubs?), and so we drove. It is a 110-mile drive from Glasgow and then a two-hour ferry ride. Within minutes of checking in, Mr M was out there wielding a club and I was unpacking in the room.

What I had not gathered from the *FT* piece was that the magical golf course is attached to a perfectly adequate but less than magical hotel. I am all for functional hotels and even stay in Formule 1 on trips across France, but for a supposedly romantic weekend away I would have preferred a place without anti-theft coathangers (I find it infuriatingly difficult to slot them into their rings), hairdryers that you have to keep the button pressed down to use (what does this do - save electricity?) and finally, worst of all, polycotton bed linen. I am 44 now, for goodness sake, and I don't expect to drive the length of England and Scotland and then be confronted with anything that has less than an 800-thread count.

The golf course, however, proved wonderful. So much so that Mr M was back out there again first thing on Saturday, and I even walked round for a few holes to reintroduce myself to him. When I eventually dragged him off to explore Islay, he had played more than 18 holes and it was the middle of the afternoon. Finally, after dinner in Port Ellen, we went back to the hotel, and I went to bed with a book under the polycotton duvet cover while he joined everyone in the bar watching the

US PGA Championship.

By the time we were back out on the course at 7.30 on the Sunday morning (yes, you read that right, 7.30am), Mr M was so in love with the place he wanted to know who owned it (Graham Lacey, who owns the Castletown course in the Isle of Man) and whether he would ever sell it. (I have no idea. Mr Lacey, if you are reading the *FT* this weekend, would you ever sell?) I think this is an unlikely Moneypenny career move, but I can tell you that if I ever become the chatelaine, there will be new coathangers, hairdryers and bed linen before Mr M can get to the first tee.

On the way up we stayed the night with my Scottish Girlfriend and her husband. Regular readers know that ScotG has been trying to educate me about classical music, so far with little success. Her latest attempt, though, may bear fruit. The Royal Scottish National Orchestra is staging some one-hour concerts at 6pm this season to fit nicely in between work and dinner out, or even I suppose, work and dinner in. An hour sounds manageable, and the three pieces on offer (Beethoven's first symphony, Brahms' first and Nielsen's fourth, all available in either Glasgow on a Thursday, or Edinburgh on a Friday), sound bearable for beginners.

ScotG is married to a former boyfriend of mine from university days, a classics scholar with a career in the arts. Waking in their house on a Friday morning was an education. ScotG remained in bed with a cup of tea, while the husband made the children's packed lunches and gave them breakfast - toast and his (yes, his) own homemade strawberry jam. Plus he doesn't listen to Radio Five Live (who cares whether Theo Walcott managed to save Arsenal's blushes during their first game in the new stadium?) and he does read the *FT*. As I said, men who read the *FT* have a certain appeal.

Facts and fuller figures

Sep 16, 2006

Mr M will be 50 at the end of the month. Earlier in the year he informed me that he did not wish to have a party; instead, he wanted to attend this year's Australian Football League grand final. So I will soon travel 12,000 miles to attend a football match. Perhaps a party would have been a better idea.

I have only ever had one husband, and so far he has lasted nearly 18 years, so just in case he has to last another 18 years I thought his 50th birthday was a good opportunity to send him off for a 100,000-mile service, namely a full medical check-up. In particular I wanted reassurance about prostate cancer (something that affects men over 50 disproportionately), body mass index (BMI) and alcohol consumption.

The BMI was to address my increasing lack of conviction that golf counts as exercise, however much you play it. Mr M walks the dog for two miles each morning, but his energy levels are still a worry. Alone overnight in the house with Cost Centre #1, who had a girlfriend visiting for the evening, Mr M was in bed and asleep before 10.30pm, waking an hour later to discover that he could still hear voices in the living room below. Thinking it was time the female guest departed, he instructed CC#1 accordingly - by text message. Clearly too much trouble to walk downstairs.

The alcohol consumption is simply a concern about the nature of Mr M's job, which, as readers know, involves the sale of vast quantities of fine wine, all of which we seem to have to try out in advance in case the clients want to know what it tastes like. He confessed to the doctor, who paled and sent his blood samples off to the lab post haste - the results show an exceptionally good liver function. Damn. I now have no reason to suggest a decrease in the consumption.

Someone who knows a thing or two about what we ought to be drinking and eating is Dame Deirdre Hutton, CBE. Dame Deirdre must occasionally be the most confused woman in the world, because she is the chair of the Food Standards Authority and the deputy chair of the Financial Services Authority. I presume the only way she knows which FSA she is at the board meeting of is if (a) she is chairing it or not and (b) it is being held in camera or not. This last because the Food Standard

Authority board meetings are held in public. Anyone can go along and attend - and they do. The agenda and papers are published in advance on the website, on which you can also watch the board meetings, if you really have nothing to do. I can't see this catching on at the other FSA, but I can imagine the delight among headhunters if it was widely adopted by public companies. "How about this Prosser chap for chairman, then?" "He might be OK - why don't I nip along to the GSK board meeting and check him out?" "Well I saw him at the Six Continents board meeting in 2003 when they discussed the Osmond bid and he was riveting," and so on. It doesn't bear thinking about.

I had lunch with Dame Deirdre and a small group of others at the City Club recently and she spoke to us about the work of the FSA - the one she chairs (www.food.gov.uk). I was a bit early, so on the way there I wandered round Tokenhouse Yard, to see what it looks like now that it is bereft of the capital markets' talent it once housed. I was half expecting a blue plaque - "David Mayhew worked here", but there isn't one. The one tenant of note was The Worshipful Company of Gardeners, so I shall be interested to see if anything grows there.

At lunch, Dame Deirdre (who is blessed with more energy and a much better BMI than I) explained that they were very concerned with obesity, and gave us the key statistics on this just as we were munching our way through our white chocolate mousse. I stopped my spoon mid-air, as did several of my fellow guests. Then, unlike several of them, I decided to munch on regardless, on the grounds that (a) I had earlier declined the bread roll and (b) white chocolate is my all-time favourite indulgence. This, however, was in clear defiance of the discussion around me of the increased incidence of type II diabetes in children, and how much it was costing the NHS to strengthen hospital beds for the obese. But I did walk down the two flights of stairs after the lunch instead of taking the lift.

I reflected afterwards on what would be a suitable birthday present for Mr M. One of the Girlfriends has just commissioned, for her boyfriend's 40th, a 5ftx3ft nude of herself reclining on a sofa from the artist Roberta Parkin, one of the more affordable executors of this genre. However, given the white chocolate mousse and other similar offences, I suspect Ms Parkin would have to order industrial quantities of oils to manage to get me on to canvas. Readers, any suggestions for an alternative present for Mr M's 50th?

It's in the posterior

Sep 23, 2006

I doubt I will ever be in need of a wealth management service. If I get to the stage where my personal free cash flow is showing a healthy surplus I know what I shall do with it: I shall buy a grouse moor.

My plaintive cry in early August that no one had invited me grouse shooting elicited exactly the response that I had hoped for, namely an invitation. It wasn't from the Queen, but you could argue that the power, influence and wealth of my host has more in common with the monarchs of 500 years ago than the ones of the present day. But I was invited to join a party on the North Yorkshire moors for two days, which was such an excitement that I cleared everything in my diary and accepted with alacrity.

North Yorkshire's only disadvantage is that it is a good four-and- a-half-hour drive from south Oxfordshire, and I knew I was going to be tired when I set off. This was because the dates were hard on the heels of the trip to the Edinburgh Fringe with Cost Centre #1 and two of his friends from school, including Profit Centre #2. GCSE results had been published four hours before this trip. I won't embarrass CC#1 by printing his results here, suffice it to say we were not dealing with the same issues as PC#2, whose greatest worry was whether he should have the one result that was not an A* re-marked.

It is an interesting experience to go to several hours of stand-up comedy with my 16-year-old son and listen to multiple jokes on the subject of oral sex, both of us wondering why the other one is laughing hysterically and knowingly. This year's

Edinburgh comedians had many themes in common with each other, and subjects that came up for ridicule and parody more than once included: Paris Hilton's new single (does she sing?); James Blunt (one act wondered whether the double negative in the song "Beautiful" - "But I won't lose no sleep on that" is an example of how badly the English language is taught at Harrow); and plastic surgery. This last reference made me particularly uncomfortable, not because I have finally summoned up the courage to go for the liposuction on my stomach that it badly needs (I haven't), but because CC#1's other accompanying friend is the son of a successful plastic surgeon. By successful, I mean someone who has found a way to recycle fat cells into school fees.

I wish I had had the liposuction before I went grouse shooting. That is because I was offered a chance to avoid the four-and-a-half-hour drive by a fellow guest who I had not met before, but who called and asked if I would like a lift in his light aircraft. The subject of weight distribution, mainly of the luggage but also of mine, came up in the conversation very soon after I accepted. Telling men I have not met before, over the telephone, how much I weigh makes me even more uncomfortable than listening to jokes about oral sex with CC#1.

We agreed to text each other on the day of travel to see if the weather was suitable. It was. My pilot then texted me to suggest that if I were prone to vomiting I should take a seasickness pill. Vomiting on someone on a first date is not something I have done since my youth, and I don't need to take drugs to prevent it.

I arrived at Thruxton Aerodrome to meet the man with whom I was going to spend the next two hours in very close quarters, squeezed inside the cockpit of a Maule MX-7. At least I was squeezed (having not been for the liposuction in advance). He was fine width-ways, being rather slim, but was quite tall - so the space constrictions were challenging in a different way. It was a rather romantic journey 2,500ft up, just him, me and a succession of increasingly stressed air-traffic controllers. An hour into the journey came a question I was even less prepared for than the one about my weight: "Is your bum hurting yet?"

My bum was not hurting, as it happens (that, I explained to him, was because of the lack of liposuction on my posterior), although as it turned out his was - a lot.

There are advantages to not being as slim as I might be. One of these, I noted as I attempted to reduce the grouse population of North Yorkshire, was almost complete protection from the recoil of the gun into my shoulder.

I enjoyed the journey there in the aircraft - the most fun I have had for ages with my clothes on - but nothing beats a day on the grouse moors with enough birds to make it satisfying, but not so many that the challenge evaporates. If I could, I would shoot grouse all through the season (August 12 to December 10) but that, I fear, would be wealth mismanagement. And, of course, I still have to pay for the liposuction.

Death in the family

Sep 30, 2006

One hundred minutes of football and a funeral. No, not the name of a new movie, but the theme of Mr M's 50th birthday visit to Melbourne.

One criticism consistently levelled against me by some who know me is that I see life through an overly optimistic lens, always expecting the best of people and events. The argument for not doing this seems to be that I can only ever be disappointed when, instead of the good things that I expect, I get a knife in the back. I admit that I am a glass half-full type of person, and my constant optimism might be construed as naive. But I prefer it that way.

Occasionally, though, something happens that makes even me realise that life is not a rehearsal. Mr M's visit to the Australian Rules Grand Final was brought forward a few days so that we could attend the funeral of a 36-year-old woman who had died in a tragic accident the week before. She was a much-loved wife, daughter, sister and aunt, but to the Moneypenny family she was something else again. She was our nanny for 10 years, on and off, from 1993 to 2003.

You might wonder why I am sharing this with you - after all, you read this column to be entertained, not depressed. But if you had known her, and anything of our relationship, you would have been entertained. Many of you have already been amused at her antics through the words of this column, especially in the very early days when I was writing it from Tokyo.

She deputised for me in much more than just maternal duties. I sent her to the earthquake planning evening at the Tokyo American Club, where she had to simulate crawling through a smoke-filled room. Looking back, I must have been very confident of her commitment to us, as it would probably have panicked any other nanny into leaving Japan immediately.

One long-running theme was her failure, in her eyes, to find the man of her dreams. She was such a gifted nanny and homemaker that it was natural that one day she would have a home and children of her own. I swung between dreading this day - because it meant she would leave - and actively trying to find some suitable candidates. One night, when Mr M was away travelling, my Most Glamorous Girlfriend and I went out drinking and ended up rather inebriated at Annabel's nightclub where I spotted quite an attractive man who was much younger than most of the assembled company. He turned out to be an opera singer called Ashley who had been entertaining a party of people at Claridge's and had come on with them to the club. I marched up and asked if he was both straight and single. He said he was, so MGG and I bundled him into a cab and took him home to meet the nanny. At 2am.

It takes a lot of alcohol to lull me into thinking that kidnapping opera singers and taking them in the early hours to be presented as a prospective husband was anything other than completely normal. Thrilled with myself, I remember my sole worry was that my nanny would be inappropriately dressed and so wouldn't immediately wow him. Marching into her bedroom my opening words were not "Sorry to disturb you, I just wondered if you would like to get up and come and meet someone." No. I cringe even now, nearly five years later, as

I relive the moment when I flung open the door, lifted up the duvet, and said with no preamble "What are you wearing?"

You couldn't be a Moneypenny nanny without learning to take my eccentricities in your stride. (Although it didn't help that she had a girlfriend, a fellow nanny, staying in her room that night, who wondered if this behaviour was normal for employers.) She got up, welcomed the bemused Ashley and offered him a cup of tea while MGG and I passed out in an alcoholic stupor. Ashley, who had no doubt thought that being annexed by two 40-year-old women in Annabel's was a precursor to something much more exciting than a cup of tea, ended up in a sleeping bag on the sofa.

Perhaps unsurprisingly, after episodes like that, she went back to Australia to take charge of her life. She became a very popular travel agent and met the man of her dreams - speed-dating, no less. Of course she explained this away by claiming that she had only gone along to keep her friend company (how many times have we all said that?) but, no matter, she went and there he was. Not one for half-measures, she got engaged in Paris and married on the beach in Fiji. I am sure that in time she would have had his children and they too would be banned, as ours were, from having Happy Meals at McDonald's (much cheaper, apparently, to buy a large chicken nugget meal and share it between them, plus no stupid plastic toys to clutter up the house).

But that wasn't to be. Instead, a few days before the 100 minutes of football, I spent rather longer with her friends and family saying our farewells. She used to love featuring in this column, and so Sally, here you are again doing what you did so well - putting a smile on people's faces. And although I can't promise to start being the parent to the Cost Centres that you were (I draw the line at handmade party decorations) I know you wouldn't have wanted me to change the way I am at all. Including, your death notwithstanding, from being a glass half-full type of person.

Diplomatic connections

Oct 07, 2006

Hair extensions baffle me. As someone who finds it hard to justify time spent going to the lavatory, you can imagine what I think about going to the hairdresser. I have long since given up visiting the salon on all but the most critical occasions, preferring to have a hairdresser come to the office so that I can work during the interminable time that it takes to put bleach through my hair.

But my (almost) newest girlfriend confessed to me the other day that she has had hair extensions put in. I was astonished. She is not married to a Premier League footballer, for goodness sake; she works in the hedge fund industry! Yet when NG turned 40 her hairdresser persuaded her to spend £600 and three hours having strands of human hair (whose?) woven into hers to increase its length. She tells me that she used the time well by having a pedicure in parallel, but I am not convinced. Plus she admits that she fiddles with her hair during meetings and the extensions fall out - not a problem that I imagine Victoria Beckham had. And they only last four months.

Hairdressers can have a disproportionate influence on people. It's all that time marooned in the chair with no one else able to offer a more balanced view. I know this because Mr M once fell so much under the spell of his hairdresser (whom he fancied) that she persuaded him to perm his hair. This was just before I met him and I have photographic evidence. He will deny it and say it was a "bodywave", but I promise you it was a perm. Another Premier League-type activity.

Many of you know that I met Mr M on an aeroplane (with permed hair), and I have recently met someone possibly even more interesting the same way. The Girlfriends are an important part of my life, and while I am not actively recruiting more I am always open to applications from suitably qualified individuals. Sitting on a flight to Edinburgh recently I noticed that across the aisle was a girl (well, a woman considerably younger than I) who was reading my column and - more importantly - laughing at it. Even after seven years of writing this column, I am still intrigued when I see someone reading it; and as she looked approachable I leant over and introduced myself.

She turned out to be fascinating, as any thirtysomething well- groomed blonde reading the *FT* on a flight to Edinburgh is likely to be. I learnt that she was from Panama, had been a postgraduate student at the LSE, and had lived and worked in the UK for several years. Speaking with a slight accent, she was, she said, a diplomat. We exchanged cards as we got off the flight, but I didn't have time to look at hers before shoving it into my handbag.

The next day, relating this story to Cost Centre #1, I extracted the card from my handbag to show him, and read it for the first time. It gave her name and, underneath, her title - Ambassador. Yes - I had been talking to Her Excellency Liliana Fernandez Puentes, Ambassador of Panama, age 36. Since when did ambassadors come in such young and attractive packages?

Now that I have learnt a little more about Panama I am not quite so surprised. For a start, the average age of the population is 26, so no wonder they have sent us a 36-year-old ambassador. Plus they have a high birth rate, so no need of Adair Turner to worry about their pension provision. But most of all, they have a canal that allows ships to pass from the Atlantic to the Pacific without having to go anywhere near the Falkland Islands. Her Excellency (to be known hereafter, I hope, as my Panamanian Girlfriend) was previously Panama's permanent delegate to the International Maritime Organisation, so she knows a thing or two about ships.

Panama sounds like a great place to visit, with a population of three million and a wide variety of geography and habitats, plus the aforementioned canal. But with no direct flights from the UK (yet - PG is so charming that I am sure she will soon have Willie Walsh agreeing to a service), it seemed rather inconvenient to nip over for a look. So I visited via the internet instead and watched a ship go through the canal - www. pancanal.com has several live webcams at strategically placed points.

The dimensions of the Panama Canal have dictated the size

of ocean-going ships for more than a century. Designing a ship that can't go through the canal is a bit like writing a computer program that isn't compatible with Windows. Panama, having finally taken over the management of its canal at the end of 1999, is considering expanding it and thus is engaging the world's shipping industry in debate. A worthwhile project, and one that will last longer than four months - and cost a little more than £600 - I am sure. Plus it is something that I understand the need for a little more than hair extensions.

Identity parade

Oct 14, 2006

Do you ever wish you were someone else? You might be forgiven for thinking that because I write this column under a pseudonym, I am really someone else, and just make up Mrs Moneypenny's life. If you fall into this category then I am sorry to disappoint you, because I really am just me, not anyone more exciting, and since starting this column more than seven years ago, every word I have written has been true.

Occasionally some of you write and ask if I am someone else. In particular, several of you have asked if I am Lucy Kellaway, the distinguished and talented *FT* staff member who writes a weekly column in the newspaper on Mondays, and a fortnightly advice column every other Wednesday. The answer, I am sad to say, is no. I am sad to say no because I frequently wish that I were Lucy Kellaway. There are numerous reasons for this, including but not limited to the fact that despite having four cost centres Ms Kellaway still possesses an enviably slim figure, and is also very fit as she cycles considerable distances to work each day. I, on the other hand, cycle not nearly as far and only have to look at spermatozoa to put on 10 kilos, so I can't imagine what I would look like if I had a fourth cost centre.

There are further differences between us, of course. One is that she is married to someone very clever, who edits the sort of magazine that is so intellectually highbrow that when you see it on someone's bedside table (as I did the other day) you look at that person in a different light. The current book on Mr M's bedside table is Beyond the Call and consists of interviews with some of Australia's best known sports commentators. Enough said.

Finally, she is a professional journalist of some 20-plus years, and I have never earned my living from writing. Just as well, I can hear some of you say. I do occasionally write feature articles under my own name, and after submitting one to the *FT* the other day the commissioning editor wrote and thanked me for my "usual accessible prose". I think we could safely translate that as indicating that I have rather a limited vocabulary.

I do sometimes wonder how different my life would be if I were another *FT* contributor. Many of you have written to me this year praising the column written by my *Weekend FT* colleague, Tyler Brule. I have never met Mr Brule, although one reader recently suggested that I interview him. Better than that, I thought, I would try and be him for a week or so. So I flew some 25,000 miles in the front end of a plane and stayed at some of the best hotels in the world, while accompanied by my laptop and some designer luggage. Like him, at my own expense.

How did I get on? Well, my suite at the Four Seasons in Hong Kong, a heartbeat away from the *FT*'s Asia offices, would have met the Tyler Brule test, with minimalist interior design and stunning views from the floor-to-ceiling glass walls that gave the impression you were almost floating over the harbour. Internet access, though, was only wireless once you had connected via a hardwire and had consented to pay HK$16 a day, which I thought Mr Brule might have found a trifle irritating.

On to Melbourne where I eschewed the big hotels and stayed at the hippest place in town, the Lyall. Here we had wireless internet access throughout the hotel, which made sitting outside in the sunshine with my laptop a joy. It was particularly handy when Cost Centre #1 called up at 9am (midnight UK time) and announced that he was lost in London. Revelries in the

King's Road had been followed by a taxi which was, he had thought, taking him to my sister's place in Clarence Road W4. Not familiar enough with London to know that King's Road to Chiswick does not involve crossing the river, he was deposited in Clarence Avenue SW4.

Armed with the wireless internet access I guided him - and a friend - from my Melbourne breakfast table across Clapham Common to Single Girlfriend's house, and she was remarkably sanguine about being woken up to take them in. He was back at school by the time I got to the next hotel, Chateau Yering, a country house extravaganza in the Yarra Valley. At dinner there I was confronted with such a complicated menu I thought I should try to be Nicholas Lander instead, and wondered whether he, too, would have been distracted by the spelling mistake on the tasting menu, where the dishes would be "there choice".

The views from the suite and some of the Yarra Valley architecture (the TarraWarra Museum of Art, designed by Allan Powell, and the Yering Station Winery, by Robert Conti) would both have passed the Brule test, and so would my next step: I ordered a helicopter from room service.

I did, really. I called reception and a Bell JetRanger (I suspect Tyler would have preferred a Dauphin) and pilot were delivered to the lawn outside our verandah. It was a magnificent way to spend the afternoon. And 1,500ft above Melbourne, once Mr M started pointing out the MCG, the Telstra Dome and all the other sports stadiums, I realised that I was still just me.

The fine art of sleeping

Oct 21, 2006

I just don't see the point of modern art. As far as I am concerned it is up there with Wagner and organic vegetables: I'm glad they exist, and am happy for those who want to consume them to do so, but I'm not going to part with any hard-earned cash in that direction.

I am aware of modern art at the periphery: I did see photos of

Tracey Emin's unmade bed and thought it quite entertaining in the way that I sometimes - though not often - find the bedroom of Cost Centre #1 quite entertaining.

I also noted Sam Taylor-Wood's video of David Beckham sleeping, which again raised a smile. I thought of making a similar video myself, of Mr M sleeping, but unless we dispensed with sound effects altogether I fear there is no sound system in the world ready to broadcast the noise of Mr M aslumber. I have tried everything - prodding him awake, and then hoping I go to sleep before him, wearing earplugs, sleeping in a different room, you name it. It got so bad last year that I packed him off to the sleep clinic in Oxford, where the NHS did the same job as Taylor-Wood for a fraction of the price.

They wired him up and videoed him snoring all night and then told him there was nothing abnormal about his sleep patterns. I obviously have a different idea of what is normal. So, I have decided, have the people who acquire works of modern art.

Last week I attended a private dinner held by London's Albion gallery in honour of the Japanese multimedia and performance artist Moriko Mori, and to show her latest installation, titled "Tom na H-iu". I had heard of the gallery and its director, Michael Hue- Williams, but never before of the artist. I was free, and thought it would be rude to refuse. (That, of course, is how I managed to get engaged so many times. You would think I had learnt my lesson.)

At my office on the afternoon of the dinner, the Lovely Lucinda presented me with the invitation and some briefing notes. To my horror, not least because I was terminally jetlagged, the dinner started at 10pm! And the installation looked, from its picture, to resemble a giant flashing condom.

Going to see a giant flashing condom before sitting down to a 10pm dinner struck me as a ludicrous use of time. I could have been tucked up in bed with a cup of tea and a copy of *The Economist*. But I had - voluntarily - accepted, and so I went.

The condom is made of glass, and is much narrower than it looks in the photos. It is exhibited in the dark, which meant you had to peer through the gloom to see if the person whose toes you were treading on was someone you knew. But the dark does allow you to appreciate the flashing LED lighting inside the condom, which is linked via the internet to a computer in the Super-Kamiokande Observatory at Tokyo university. The computer detects the presence of neutrinos arriving from outer space; this information is translated by the sculpture into changing patterns of coloured light (no, I am not making this up).

Having stood in the dark and interacted with outer space, I moved back into the light and across to the other part of the gallery for dinner. As I walked in I noticed a large, clear, acrylic box sitting to one side. What, I asked, was that? It was, I was told, Ms Mori's pod. Her pod? She apparently lies down in it in different parts of the world with her eyes closed, and is filmed doing so - though not, I suspect, by Sam Taylor-Wood or, indeed, the NHS.

Now I can understand the need for the occasional kip, and the pod looked perfectly comfortable, but to lie around in a plastic box in Piccadilly Circus dressed in brightly coloured underwear and to be filmed doing so strikes me as a little odd.

I was most definitely in the minority, I discovered. The other 200 plus people at the dinner all loved the condom - and the pod - and were quite happy eating at 10pm because they had all been out freezing somewhere - or that's what I thought they said. It sounded a bit unlikely, as we were having the warmest October on record, but then it turned out they had all been at Frieze, which I now know is an annual modern art fair.

But I found a few reasons to recommend the Albion gallery, even if flashing condoms are not your thing. For a start, Mr Hue-Williams doesn't exhibit at Frieze, so you can't see his gallery's stuff anywhere else (probably just as well, because the flashing condom is enormous and I can't see how anyone could transport it anywhere). The gallery also employs its own Michelin-starred chef, who turns out the most fabulous food, even for more than 200 people at 10 o'clock at night. But most important for us girls, Mr H-W is drop-dead gorgeous and wears immaculately tailored suits. I would happily pay to watch him asleep - fully dressed - in a pod any day. Indeed, that would be modern art that I could quite see the point of.

Night terrors

Nov 18, 2006

At this time of the year I frequently sleep in strange beds. And Mr M is rarely in them with me.

Not that anyone else is there, you understand. The reason for the bed hopping is that we are in the thick of the shooting season and this frequently, but not always, involves an overnight stay. There is usually dinner the night before the shoot, as an opportunity to meet and bond with your fellow guests before venturing forth the next day with loaded gun.

This season I have graced the sheets of a pub in North Yorkshire, a manor house in Hampshire and a castle in Scotland. It can be tricky to know what to wear - not to shoot, or to dinner, but to bed. But who is going to see you? I can hear you ask.

In fact many people may see you in your nightwear on these trips. This is because you are often staying in people's homes. This is a great honour, particularly as these tend to be large and historic, but you cannot rely on there being that invention that came very late to these shores - the en suite bathroom.

The lack of en suite bathrooms in British stately homes results in real issues of nightwear selection, and the castle in Scotland was an excellent example of this. Eight of us stayed the night, which was fine as it has many more bedrooms than that. Only one bedroom, however, had an en suite bathroom and that was naturally allocated to the American among us. I was therefore required to go along a corridor to the nearest bathroom, which made waking at 3am and needing the loo an event that brought on a moment of wardrobe panic. Along the same corridor were sleeping three CEOs of public companies in the Eurofirst 300. Would my nightdress (satin, pale blue, five years old, floor-length from M&S) be up to meeting one of them? And worse, what would they be wearing? Would I be able to look them in the eye the next day without blushing if I had encountered a gaping pair of pyjama trousers?

Of course, back in the days when these houses hosted great shooting parties, the guests (or their butlers) packed their dressing gowns. I do possess a dressing gown but taking it with me would double the space requirement, and there is quite enough stuff that needs taking on a shooting engagement without having to add to it, especially if you are flying with some low-cost airline that charges for luggage. It is easier, I think, just to upgrade my nightwear. Mr M has raised an eyebrow as I have recently sallied forth to acquire new and more glamorous outfits for sleeping in at shoots.

Mr M may yet benefit from my acquisitions. From time to time, I go on shoots where partners are invited. One of these, at Belvoir Castle, is coming up. I have never stayed at Belvoir before and have no idea how many of the bedrooms have ensuite bathrooms, but I will pack the new nightie just in case.

Mr M and I are delighted to be invited to Belvoir as corporate guests and Mr M especially is looking forward to being a corporate spouse there. A reader wrote in recently to ask how it was that my marriage had lasted for 18 years, as from my column I seemed to have little in common with my spouse. Please, she said, just for once, could I pen a few words on how wonderful he was, rather than mentioning yet again how he spends all his time drinking wine and playing golf? Well, he is a wonderful corporate spouse, not least because he is ready and willing to chat to anyone else's spouse abut anything. His willingness to come to Belvoir is evidence of this. I am told that spouses on this shoot have a separate schedule, allowing them to have breakfast in bed and a tour of the castle before joining the guns for lunch. This is much more appealing than having to drag themselves out into the rain and stand behind the peg saying "well shot" at regular intervals. Driving all the way to Leicestershire to have breakfast in bed is probably not on Mr M's list of things to do with a precious day off work, and so I am very grateful to him. There you are - a good word about Mr M. Although I am sure he will drink plenty of wine at the dinner and if they can't find him when they deliver the breakfast, I suspect he will be on the nearest golf course.

More strange bedrooms beckon as I am shooting every week between now and Christmas. One of these is a "blind shoot" - the equivalent of a "blind date" as I have accepted an invitation to shoot with an *FT* reader I have never met, and in whose bed I have never slept. If the column doesn't appear after next week, please alert the police in Suffolk.

The best shooting bedroom of all, though, in recent weeks, has been in an elegant country house where the host gave up his bedroom for me. With his family away on half term, he slept in the children's room in a sacrificial gesture. I loved the bed, with Egyptian cotton sheets, and I needed satellite navigation to find my way across acres of floor to the (en suite) bathroom. I set my alarm on my mobile telephone for 0730 - as opposed the usual 0600. Later, as we left for the shoot, I noticed my phone was missing. After a weekend fruitlessly looking for it I had to get the Lovely Lucinda to call our host's office and explain that I thought it was in his bed - which it was.

Cosmetic damage

Nov 25, 2006

Leonardo da Vinci has a lot to answer for. When he published his plans for a flying machine, he might not have realised it but more than 500 years later he cost me £99.50 in lost cosmetics.

The UK has just relaxed slightly the restrictions on flying with liquids. But when I flew to Scotland recently for a shoot, all restrictions were still in force. Having sent my luggage and my gun up by road, I thought I had done everything to speed my way through Stansted, including taking only one piece of hand luggage. This had forced me to cram my Anya Hindmarch handbag into my laptop case, which was a terrible thing to do (and here's hoping Anya doesn't read this). Had you seen me you would have signed up to the League Against Cruelty to Handbags - Anya's bags are not designed to be emptied on the train to Stansted and then folded up and squashed into the space alongside a laptop.

For all its cruelty, the consolidation worked and I was let through the first security check, only to be accosted after my bag had been through the X-ray machine. A stern-looking woman walked towards me. Naturally I thought she was going to lecture me on the perils of squashing a £500 handbag into a space not designed for the purpose, but no, it was far worse than that. I had my make-up in the side pocket, and much of it was liquid.

Into the bin went the Lancome Definicils mascara (£17.50), followed closely by the Elizabeth Arden Flawless Finish Radiant Moisture Make-up (£18) and the YSL Touche Eclat Radiant Touch (£22). This last was especially galling as it doubles as both spot concealer and something to hide the bags under my eyes. Both are essential for shooting expeditions, which invariably involve a late and boozy dinner, hence the bags. I know that if I presented my true complexion to the birds the next day they would all fly in the opposite direction. Quite why I still get spots at 44 years of age puzzles me. When do they stop? At 50? Sixty? Is it something that the menopause will cure?

When the security official took out an almost full 50ml bottle of 24 Faubourg eau de parfum by Hermes (£42), I swallowed hard and said that if I couldn't take it on board, the bin was a shocking place for it to go and why didn't she take it with her at the end of her shift and give it a good home? But it was an offer that fell on deaf ears.

By the time all this had been played out I was perilously close to missing the flight, which was boarding at the furthest gate from security. I assume that the further the gate, the lower the landing charge, and as I was using an airline run by Michael O'Leary I should have expected this. Shoes had to be removed and X-rayed too, and I didn't bother putting them back on. Leonardo designed many useful things, but they didn't include a pair of heels that allow you to run to gate 92 at Stansted airport without breaking your neck.

I arrived breathless and shoeless with face (and therefore

spots) glowing in the boarding queue next to a senior investment banker who was a fellow shooting guest. This was not the impression I had been aiming for. Making an impression when shooting is harder than you think. It helps to shoot like a dream of course, but as my enthusiasm for the sport way exceeds my skill I try to make an impression in other ways. One thing I try to do is to make sure I have the right clothes. But after arriving at a shoot recently, I was installed in a very smart bedroom by my host who stood and chatted to me as I unpacked. But as I laid out my sweater for the next day I heard a sharp intake of breath. "Mrs M, are you sure that is your colour? Come with me," he said, and led me to his dressing room where there was a cupboard filled floor to ceiling with cashmere shooting jerseys in various shades of green. He fished out one of them and handed it to me. He is a client, so I thought that I had better wear it, but I find the concept of heterosexual - and happily married - men showing an interest in what I wear as puzzling as having spots at 44.

I wore the sweater the next day and had hoped to keep it, but I got the impression he expected it to be returned, so my assistant the Lovely Lucinda sped it straight to the cleaners.

What this man does have, of course, as well as a myriad of shooting jerseys, is the use of a private aircraft. Having your own aeroplane has definite appeal, not least so that I can take my gun and my spot concealer with me at all times without having to queue to go through security. I have therefore enrolled to study for my private pilot's licence exams, and am just finishing that gripping tome Air Law and Operational Procedures, before moving on to the sequel Navigation and Meteorology. Not quite as easy a read as The Da Vinci Code, but all inspired by the same person. As I said, Leonardo's got a lot to answer for.

Mother of all bad examples

Dec 02, 2006

Parenting is not my strongest skill set. I have bemoaned my inadequacies in this area many times in these pages, and, each time I do so, many of you kindly write in with suggestions of books to read, or ideas about how I might improve.

Not as many of you, however, as have written in to suggest places I might buy appropriate nightwear to take to shooting parties where I am likely to sleep in a room without an en suite bathroom. My description of the terror of waking at 3am and debating with myself the relative benefits of bladder control versus the risk of being sighted in dubious nightwear and no make-up prompted many of you to send in suggestions for items of clothing that, as one reader put it, "wouldn't frighten the dogs". These were all extremely welcome, even the one from an ex-boyfriend who sent me a hyperlink to a cashmere dressing gown that looked very glamorous, but had a suitably glamorous price, too. He is a successful businessman with several thousand acres to his name, and I guess he seems to have forgotten that I didn't marry him (he asked someone else). If I had, maybe cashmere dressing gowns at £395 might be standard purchases.

With three cost centres (or four if you include the dog who is still away at gun-dog boarding school at the cost of a cashmere dressing gown a month), clothes shopping is not high on the agenda. The Moneypenny family does occasionally scrape together the money, however, to go on family outings. One such recently was to see Nicholas Hytner's film *The History Boys*. The reason for this was not only that it was an acclaimed play and film written by Alan Bennett, but also that CC#1 was an extra in it and appears on screen for all of 30 seconds or so.

What I had not realised, and did not check beforehand, was that *The History Boys* is classed as a 15. This meant that CC#2 (age 12) and CC#3 (age seven) were not allowed in. Standing at the ticket office, with 10 minutes to go, I made a snap decision. I bought the two younger boys tickets to see some animated film about a bear that was starting at almost the same time. Just as they were about to depart for their seats, thrilled at this turn of events that saw them escape from thought-provoking scenes about the real role of education in life to unsupervised non-stop cartoon characters, I thought to ask what time their film finished. Forty minutes before ours, I was informed. Without another thought I reached into my wallet and found a £5 note. I issued it to CC#2 and instructed him to buy sweets after the film finished and to use them to keep him and his brother occupied in gum decay while waiting for us to emerge from the screen next door.

It didn't occur to me until later that abandoning my two youngest children in a strange cinema at a moment's notice, and then bribing them with sweets to wait 40 minutes for us to take them home might not have been regarded as the best parenting decision in the world. I was reminded of a question asked of me recently by a BBC interviewer. To what, they had inquired, did I attribute the "extraordinary independence and self sufficiency" of my children? Easy, I said. Neglect.

One thing I have neglected to do as a parent, in respect of CC#3, is speak to him about sex. I managed this with CC#1 at seven years old and CC#2 (I think) at eight, both just before they were about to be outsourced to boarding school. (The cost of this, by the way, could dress the population of a small African nation in cashmere dressing gowns, although I guess they might be a bit warm.) I am not sure how good I or many other parents are at tackling this subject, so I was interested to have the opportunity recently to read the booklets issued by the Family Planning Association, and to learn of its programme, Speakeasy, which aims to help parents through the process.

I offered them to CC#2 to preview. He told me he knew it all already, but then came back after reading them and asked me what a tampon was, which must be a result of living in a house full of boys.

Even CC#3, when asked if he would like me to explain about the birds and the bees, told me not to bother. He had, he informed me, had it all explained to him by his eldest brother. I dread to think what he told him, but at least it has saved me from having to do so. Parenting, as I said, is not one of my strongest skills.

Fat chance

Dec 09, 2006

Gifts are a conundrum – as defined in the Merriam-Webster Online Dictionary as - "an intricate and difficult problem".

Don't get me wrong, I love the process of giving - and receiving - gifts. And this time of year is a great opportunity to indulge in doing so. It is just that the issue of what to give, and to whom, is preying on my mind. I find myself making lists in the back of my notebook during business meetings and then wondering where I will find the time to go and get all the items listed.

At the office we have for some years adopted the so-called "Secret Santa" system. Everyone draws a name out of a hat and then has to buy a present costing less than £10 (which is refunded by the company) for whomever they have drawn. On the day of our Christmas lunch we ceremonially open these presents one by one and see who has managed to buy the most original and amusing gift for the randomly selected recipient. The pressure to outdo each other in originality and amusement grows each year, and so I have been wrestling with what to get for my recipient, which certainly is an intricate and difficult problem.

As if that wasn't bad enough, my in-laws have now decided to go in for this practice. Christmas this year will be spent 12,000 miles away. Rationalising why we are flying five of us 12,000 miles at the most expensive time of the year to spend quality time with my mother-in-law is an even more intricate and difficult problem. My sister-in-law, in whose establishment we will be celebrating Christ's birth, has sent a full agenda and menus for our stay, including an instruction that we should only buy presents for the children of the family. Adults will be allocated a single random recipient, in the same manner as takes place at my office. I have drawn my brother-in-law and my husband his father. I have no idea what we shall purchase for them, but I am not so worried about that as the intricate and difficult problem of deciding what our children are going to perform at the family concert on Christmas Eve. I find watching my own children give public performances excruciating at the best of times, so how I am going to find watching my nieces and nephews, I cannot think.

What I really want for Christmas is £5,000 worth of liposuction. I have thought this for some time, but the final confirmation came when exercising under the harsh regime of Holly the Sadist, who puts me through my paces in the gym each week. At one point HTS looked me up and down and then, after some thought and consulting her notebook, said with a decisive tone, "15 kilos". I immediately agreed with her and promised that I would try to lose 15 kilos as soon as possible. She looked at me in exasperation and then pointed out that she was deciding what weight to give me to bench press.

HTS has received a jolly nice gift recently - a substantial square-cut diamond. This was from her boyfriend, when he asked her to be his wife. For some reason the marriage is going to be in 2008. I am all for diamonds as gifts, but what is it with long engagements? I just don't see the point. I was a serial fiancée, getting engaged four times, and frankly it wasn't so great an experience that I needed it to go on for 18 months at a stretch. And I don't care what people say about engagements being a time of preparation for marriage; nothing prepares you for picking someone's laundry off the bedroom floor for 18 years and more.

In the meantime, HTS is sporting the diamond, which has forced her to take the time to have a proper manicure. She rather begrudges the cost of a manicure but I maintain that this is completely unreasonable. Any girl who is given a substantial diamond ring owes it to the donor to spend £20 every now and again to show it off; peeling nail varnish is too tacky for words.

On the same principle I should really buy a Wellington boot bag to house my £200 wellies instead of carting them around in a bin liner. (Mr M, if you are reading this, and the liposuction is a tad expensive, I would like a John Chapman Wellington boot bag for Christmas. That's given him the solution to an intricate and difficult problem.) Other suggestions for him and/or the Cost Centres are new shooting gloves (I left my mittens behind on a shoot earlier in the season and it has just become cold enough to miss them), some pink shooting socks and some suitably expensive hand cream (to combat the damage done by all those shoots I have been on recently without gloves).

And what am I going to get for Mr M? And the Girlfriends? (This last would be easier if the shops in the West End stocked a variety of solvent, single and heterosexual men.) Gifts are indeed an intricate and difficult problem. Or in other words, a conundrum.

Scents and sensibility

Dec 16, 2006

Christmas can be full of surprises - and the surprise for me this year is that I am not having any time off. The Moneypenny activities will continue to be printed in another part of the *FT* at the weekend even though the magazine will get some time off. The *FT* has in fact delivered several surprises over the year: they managed, for instance, on my birthday to publish a large picture of Anshu Jain, the very dishy head of markets at Deutsche Bank.

But the biggest (and best) surprise that I received via the *FT* recently was an invitation to shoot as the guest of a reader in East Anglia. I set off, train ticket booked by the Lovely Lucinda, to have dinner and spend the night with total strangers. I am pleased to report that I returned alive and having had a great time, not least because my hosts were very hospitable. No en suite bathroom, but there was a dressing gown in the room on arrival (and the guest in the next door room, with whom I was sharing a bathroom, was a suitably gorgeous man, so dressing gown possibly slightly optional if we both hadn't been married).

After dinner I withdrew to take a bath, an appealing idea at the end of a long day. My hostess urged me to take advantage of all the pampering luxuries that she had put in the bathroom, and I noticed that these included a rather splendid-looking dual-wicked scented candle. I am not usually a scented-candle kind of girl, but it struck me that it might be just the thing to have a relaxing aroma wafting past me in the bath, and so I lit it, before returning to the bedroom to fetch my wash bag.

On my return, two minutes later, the scented candle had expanded its flame beyond its dual wicks to the whole surface of the wax, and black smoke was billowing up the tiles and on to the pale blue wall. In a panic I shut the bathroom door, grabbed the candle and opened the window, frantically blowing the flame out in the process and spilling burning wax on to my trigger finger. Without thinking, I grabbed the towel (white - my hosts have no cost centres - have you noticed that people without children often have white towels?), wet it and wiped down the wall. The end result was a towel that looked as though I had used it to remove my mascara for the past three days. As I was in too much pain to go to sleep, I sat up in bed with my fingers in a glass of water, and read one of the books my hosts had thoughtfully placed in my room. English Barometers, 1680-1860, by Nicholas Goodison, has lots of pictures, and I can recommend it for pyromaniacs who have trouble sleeping. I was intrigued by the book because, up until then, my knowledge of Sir Nicholas was as a former chairman of the Stock Exchange and TSB, rather than as a noted barometer expert.

The next morning, rather tired and clutching a blackened towel, but fully conversant with the knowledge that a barometer is an instrument that measures the weight of the air, I ventured downstairs. The rest of the day was spent shooting in convivial company, and the only further surprise was that I managed to hit anything.

The first two drives passed by with my discharging a total of four cartridges and failing to trouble the scorer at all. My host, who wasn't shooting on the line himself, clearly decided after this inauspicious start that I needed a bit of help, came and stood with me on the third drive and gave a lot of coaching involving straight left arms and legs and feet that needed, in his opinion, moving around a bit. As I have said in these pages before, if men gave women as much detailed instruction in bed as they do on the sports field, we'd all be much better off.

Fortunately for both of us, I did start hitting things from then on, even with a blister developing on my trigger finger. I say fortunately because, although I love hearing from readers, I always worry that I am going to be a great disappointment to them in the flesh. Inviting a random *FT* columnist to a shoot and then finding that she is a fully paid up member of the East Anglian Game Bird Preservation Society could be the wrong kind of surprise for a *FT* reader.

What a Bastion

23 December 2006

The British are not bad at castles. We have quite a few of them of all shapes and sizes, ranging from the very large (Windsor) to the very small (Bodiam). Anyone can buy one and they do. And if you can't afford to buy one or have better things to do with your money, you can rent one for the weekend.

If you fancy this, then I commend to you the website www.lhhscotland.com, which I happened on when booking the Moneypenny family holiday for summer 2007. I was tempted by, but resisted, a castle that came complete with dungeon - somewhere to put the cost centres (or indeed the husband) if they behave badly.

Recently it has been me who nearly had to be put in the dungeon. Mr M and I were guests last month at Belvoir Castle a gothic pile near Grantham, Lincolnshire, where we were entertained by the wealth management division of a Swiss bank. Our host has a worldwide advertising campaign with the strapline "You and us", presumably to reinforce the personal nature of their service. Well, for this particular outing it was more like "You, us, a few other guests and their Graces the Duke & Duchess of Rutland".

It was unsurprising that the Rutlands showed up as Belvoir is their home. It's a sizeable pad, with all the amenities one might look for in a piece of real estate if you have five children, as the Rutlands do - chapel, ballroom, 15,000 acres and so on. Although the castle is built on a hill with a stunning view (hence Belvoir), its name is pronounced "beaver", as in Creek. Don't ask me why. There are some questions in life that stump me.

Their Graces hosted us to a slap-up dinner in their state dining room. My last words to Mr M the week before on the subject of this dinner had been to assure him that it would not be black tie. Who still has black tie shooting dinners midweek in November these days? The Rutlands, it turns out. Having established this rather late in the day (through finally reading the instructions) I was delegated to pack Mr M's dinner suit as he had left it in London.

I also packed his proper bow tie, which after 18 years of marriage he still cannot tie. Therefore, he can only wear it when attending functions with me, who can. What I did forget, however, were the trousers. This only came to light as we were dressing for dinner in the cavernous and elegantly appointed bedroom that the Duke of Wellington had used regularly when visiting a previous generation of Rutlands. (Before you ask, it did have an ensuite bathroom and also a scented candle that I refrained from lighting). If Belvoir had had a dungeon, I would have been in it.

After exchanging some terse words with me on my inadequacies as a wife (or rather, as a valet), Mr M decided to wear his navy moleskins, which come from RM Williams and are heavily branded. The length of the dinner jacket hid the branding and the dim lighting of the Belvoir staterooms hid the rest. With such a vast home, the Rutlands would be bankrupted by the electricity bill if they switched on all the lights and I was impressed to see Emma Rutland switching them off wherever she went.

In fact, I was quite impressed with Emma Rutland altogether. While I am not actively looking for new girlfriends, she has many of the qualities that would commend her to the list. You can find out a lot about Her Grace the Duchess of Rutland on the internet, in the Belvoir Castle guide book and so on (such as she's a year younger than me and possessed of a much more enviable figure) but I bet I found out a few things that most people wouldn't know.

Who is aware, for instance, that she does the school run from time to time in diamante Jimmy Choos, especially on evenings when she has black tie shooting dinners? Doing the school run at all slightly horrifies me but as only one Rutland Cost Centre is outsourced to boarding school (not entirely unreasonable, as they range in age from 13 to three), there are a few school runs to fit in.

And, to keep the heating bill down, she wears her winter coat to dinner, which she is likely to have bought in Sign of the Times, off Chelsea Green, where she shops for second-hand designer clothes. Finally, her first name is Rachael - Emma is her middle name. Why do parents give their children perfectly good first names and then use a different one? Another unanswerable question, I suspect.

Emma, Rachael, whatever, displayed a great sense of humour, enormous energy and an infinite capacity for multi-tasking, all qualities I would look for in a DG, or ducal girlfriend. Belvoir opens to the public in 2007 on April 3 so, for the price of an admission ticket (£11), you might be able to meet her too. If you prefer to look at something older and wider than Her Grace, they have a rather striking Holbein portrait of Henry VIII. As well as a collection of armoury and weapons to delight the heart of any small boy. As I said, the British are not bad at castles.

On sturdy ground

30 December 2006

One million pounds. No, this is not the sum of money that I earn each year. Neither is it the cost of raising three cost centres (I imagine it is much greater than that). It is the cost of our 10-year lease on the office, though. And it is the amount by which I have been told my life is underinsured.

Personally I thought that I had so much life insurance that

I couldn't possibly need any more. But the experts say that although all our debt would be paid off if I meet an untimely end, Mr M would have nothing to live on or to pay the nanny and the cleaner. Quite why Mr M would need to employ a nanny or a cleaner, I do not know. He could, presumably, marry another one. He is, after all, quite presentable, gainfully employed and could maybe upgrade to include golf-playing on the next Mrs M model. Indeed, she might play golf but not clean as he could keep the current cleaner. Our cleaner is from the Philippines - quite exotic in Oxfordshire but very common in London and almost universal in Hong Kong. Overseas remittances to the Philippines from the army of cleaners, nurses and drivers round the world come to more than Dollars 4bn annually. That's a lot of cleaning, even at the £10 an hour that we pay.

So, back to this million pounds, presumably to allow Mr M to pay for the cleaner in case his looks have deserted him by then and/or he is too busy playing golf to find someone else to marry. To insure my life for a sum of this magnitude requires an insurance medical, this time at some grubby rooms in Harley Street with peeling paint where you wonder if they had ever had a cleaner, Filipino or otherwise. After a barrage of questions from the secretary in her cramped office, I move into the consulting room and answer another barrage from the doctor. Have I ever been in hospital for anything other than childbirth? No. What do I do? I am a company director. Oh, and I write a national newspaper column, teach on an MBA programme and am raising three cost centres and a husband. Am I pregnant? I hope not. As Mr M had a vasectomy six years ago, I could have some explaining to do.

After all the questions, the moment of truth - I am put on the scales. The doctor looks at the reading and then there is some sucking in of breath followed by the comment "My my, we are a sturdy lass". A sturdy lass! Why doesn't he just come right out with it and say that I am fat? My height is then pronounced to be 5ft 3in and there is more sucking in of breath while we look up my Body Mass Index on the chart to see if I am in the section coloured bright red. What would this indicate, I ask? That I am "morbidly obese", I am told. Fortunately I am not morbidly obese but we do mention three or more times again how "sturdy" I am.

The tape measure then comes out and what used to be called my vital statistics are measured to see if my waist is smaller than my hips. This is apparently required to know if I am more or less likely to have a heart attack. I am very dubious when the doctor measures my chest and even more alarmed when he asks me to remove my clothes and lie on the examination couch. He did at this stage call in the nurse, who was not Filipino but looked slightly worried, presumably in case the rather ancient examination couch gave way under the sturdy lass lying on it.

After prodding my chest, supposedly for lumps, the doctor then inspected the scars from the entry into this world of the three cost centres. Was that strictly necessary? I didn't think it was the right moment to ask what he thought of the handiwork of my latest discovery, Lulu in Marylebone High Street. Mind you, it's not cheap, all this waxing. Once Mr M has paid the cleaner, bought his new wife a set of golf clubs and paid for her beauty treatments he might need the million pounds.

After getting dressed, I am subjected to yet more questions about my medical history. Have I ever consulted a psychiatrist? No is the answer, although if I have to endure much more of this medical I am thinking that I might need to. I am just starting to think that it might be less traumatic if I remained underinsured and Mr M put up with a dirty house when I am mercifully released from the ordeal.

I await to see if my premiums, estimated to be £155 a month, are to be loaded for being too fat. Personally I think they should be discounted to compensate me for the grubby doctor and the peeling paint, not to mention the caesarean scar inspection. And being told that I am a sturdy lass. My reaction was to go straight to a shop and buy a large assortment of Green & Blacks chocolate to share with everyone in the office. Our office is very nice, clean (because we have a daily cleaner who is Japanese, which is exotic anywhere) and doesn't have peeling paint. Well worth a million pounds.

Cheap at half the price

Jan 06, 2007

India is high on my agenda for 2007. No, I am not moving there. I have visited many times, initially as a child and later when bankers and brokers were beating down the doors of the place in the mid-1990s. It's a fascinating country, both from an economic and a cultural perspective, and one that I hope to visit again in the future.

But India is on my mind for other reasons as we enter the New Year. In December I had breakfast with one of the Girlfriends, a smart Antipodean who is an IT entrepreneur. She told me that she had outsourced her back office operations - four people who had earned about £30,000 each - to India, where she is paying $25 a day per person for an excellent five-man project team instead. Technology Entrepreneur Girlfriend spoke in glowing terms of the professionalism and performance levels of this team who were undertaking routine administrative tasks several thousand miles from her office, to great effect and at minimum cost.

This has given me a thought - why don't I outsource my assistant, the Lovely Lucinda? Although no one in our office earns like Goldman Sachs partners, they certainly cost more than $25 a day. Looking at her main routine tasks - my travel arrangements, my expenses, booking shooting days, calling the taxi company to recover my BlackBerry or other abandoned items - all these could be done easily on the internet or by telephone from New Delhi, where TEG's project team is based. Think of the saving!

I have tested out this idea on several of my colleagues. They have pointed out that while all of the above tasks could be managed from India, there are a few that might be trickier to achieve. Such as? The purchase of emergency pairs of tights before crucial client meetings when I have managed to rip my own pair to shreds with 30 minutes to go was cited. Why? LL (or the $25 a day version) could call John Lewis or log on to www.mytights.com and have them biked round. Who would collect my dry cleaning? Easy - there's a delivery service. Decorating the Christmas tree, which LL has done superbly this year, is another task that my colleagues suggest might be harder to accomplish from New Delhi. I disagree. The cut-price LL could order a fully decorated tree complete with lights straight off the internet.

There isn't much that an outsourced LL could not achieve from India, as there is so much you can do on the web these days - even ordering your passport. Having had to get a passport issued in double-quick time a year ago I shall not be needing another one until 2016, unless of course I leave it in the back of a taxi. My Most Glamorous Girlfriend, however, does need another passport. Hers has fewer than six months to run, to which many countries object. This hasn't bothered her much until recently, when she had a couple of dates with an eligible single man, and in the manner of Bridget Jones her mind has turned to the possibility that he might ask her on a mini-break. If the mini-break were to be overseas, she might not be able to go.

I have pointed out that the jump from a drink and a dinner to a mini-break might take a while yet, but MGG is having none of it. She has been to get her passport photo done. Three times. Yes, three separate visits, the last two of which were preceded by a visit to the hairdresser. At this rate I think that the man running Snappy Snaps in Shepherd's Market in Mayfair is going to think that she fancies going on a mini-break with him.

Still, if I were single and in search of a third husband I guess I might be fussy about my passport photo. I am of course still married to my first husband, but I shall be outsourcing him to India soon, in February. He is going there on a cricket tour for two weeks. Two weeks travelling round India playing cricket interspersed with some serious drinking, or possibly the other way around, at the age of 50 in the middle of the school term sounds like a jolly to me. How I am going to manage without him for a fortnight I do not know. I may cave in and go over there to seek him out for part of the trip.

Indeed seeking husbands in India seems to me to be much more straightforward than it is here. Instead of panicking about passport photos and mini-breaks you can just advertise in the newspapers or find someone to organise an arranged marriage for you. This strikes me as very sensible. Perhaps a trip to India would be a more worthy reason for renewing MGG's passport if she is serious about the third husband.

LL had a brief starter marriage some time ago but has been single ever since. She did not look too happy when I told her that I was considering outsourcing her to India, at least until I explained about the availability of arranged marriages. Then she seemed up for it. A married LL might even be so happy that she would be prepared to work for $25 a day in New Delhi. India, I suggest, may be a popular destination in 2007.

Bags me the first class flight

Jan 13, 2007

Commercial air travel can be tedious. The Moneypenny family travelled to Australia over the Christmas holidays, courtesy of an airline with a kangaroo on its tail. Mr M went first, accompanied by the three cost centres, reflecting the facts that (a) he can take more holiday than me and (b) it is his country, so he wants to spend longer there. From one perspective, Australia is the most fabulous holiday destination on earth. From another, it is a woefully underpopulated country where it is almost impossible to make any serious money. A group of people hoping that the former view will help them to disprove the latter is the team taking the kangaroo airline private in an A$12bn deal. That sounds big until you convert it to UK£.

I drove the Moneypenny team to their appointment with the pre- Christmas Heathrow chaos. They checked in six pieces of luggage; a suitcase each, a bag of revision for Cost Centre #1's AS levels, and Mr M's golf clubs. Only one piece arrived. The golf clubs.

From one perspective, Mr M's, this showed that the baggage

handlers had their priorities right. From another, namely mine, 12,000 miles away, it was a massive inconvenience. This was because Mr M, faced with the prospect of playing golf in the clothes he flew out in, took the type of resourceful action that he always does in a crisis - he called me.

Several telephone calls by me later (to BAA, British Airways and then American Express, our insurers), I was able to tell Mr M that he could go out and spend A$6,000 on clothes. That is big even when you convert it to UK£.

Cost Centre #1 thought that Santa Claus had arrived a few days early. Not only had any danger of exam revision been removed by the loss of his schoolwork bag, but he was also given carte blanche to go out and spend money on clothes. Mr M, on the other hand, dislikes shopping for clothes with children, and so between them they managed a paltry A$2,400.

I flew to Sydney a few days later. This caused some comment, because although I flew on the same airline, I flew first class - the earlier party had been made to travel at the back of the aeroplane. I make no apologies for this. Children, in my opinion, should not be allowed to travel anything other than economy, unless they can pay for it themselves. Small children make a noise and annoy me - if you can afford to fly your children at the front of the plane, you can afford to pay for someone to travel with them at the back of the plane. Larger children, on the other hand, are being ruined by their parents' largesse. A whole generation is growing up with no appreciation of the value of money because, among other things, their parents are flying them round the world in first and business class.

Presumably the key people taking Qantas private are hoping to make enough money to fly themselves and their children first class, or even better, by private jet, for ever. But I just don't get it. The deal will be leveraged to the hilt in the usual manner of these things. Where are they going to get the improvement in performance needed to pay it all back? What will they sell? And to whom? And whatever they do, surely it won't be anything that a competent and properly incentivised management team couldn't have done under public ownership? They are even keeping the same CEO, Geoff Dixon - couldn't he have managed whatever rabbit he is going to pull out of whichever hat as a public company? Margaret Jackson, Qantas's chairman, and her board, have missed a trick, in my opinion. They will pass into the history books as having got the offer increased from A$5.50 to A$5.60 (which, in any currency, is an increase of less than 2 per cent) rather than seizing the opportunity to become the heroes of the institutional investor community. Qantas will be refloated or sold in a few years and a small number of investors will make a large amount of money. Had the board delivered the same performance improvement under public ownership many more people would have been able to share in the gains.

Despite the leaf tea served in Qantas first class (what a pain for the cabin crew to wash up) they don't offer Krug, an omission that I hope will be addressed once the new owners of the airline take possession. Not least because a non-executive director of Allco Finance Group, which will be the largest shareholder, is Sir Rod Eddington, who has previously run both Cathay Pacific and British Airways, both of which serve Krug in first class. They also have far nicer pillowcases.

Sir Rod is also a non-executive of News Corporation. Here he has Rupert Murdoch as chairman. Mr Murdoch famously used to travel between New York and London by commercial airline, in the days when Concorde was still in service. He did, of course, have access to a private jet, but it wasn't supersonic so took longer. Instead it crossed the Atlantic, carrying his luggage. Which would certainly have ensured that it all arrived.

Call that a shop sign?

Jan 20, 2007

Families cause stress. That's my opinion, anyway. Christmas and New Year are when I see my family for the longest non-stop period in the year and it usually shows. I love Mr M and the Cost Centres dearly, but after organising a four-centre, three-week visit to Australia I was ready to get back to the office for respite.

Where to go for our annual family holiday is always a subject of debate. Finding somewhere that appeals to all the Cost Centres (who are now 17, 12 and eight), while having sufficient wine stocks and golf courses to keep Mr M happy, is not as easy as it was. A reader called Tim suggested that we go on a safari. "Perhaps a bonding trip with your cost centres would contribute another life-enhancing experience to your column? Seeing predators in short grass can do wonders for family dialogue."

Well, Tim, I have news for you - we saw quite a lot of predators in short grass during our family holiday, including one in particular called Shane Warne. This did do wonders for family dialogue, especially as everyone in the family other than me carries an Australian passport. The dialogue became so strong on the subject of England's failure to challenge Australia's supremacy on the cricket field that I felt compelled to leave them to it at one stage during the Melbourne Test, and went handbag shopping instead.

The language barrier in Australia still defeats me on occasion. I was planning to hit the sales, which were heavily advertised in the press. Every department store took out double-page spreads, and in some cases billboards on the major highways, alerting shoppers to the savings to be made in various departments, including outdoor furniture, womenswear and Manchester. Manchester? They have whole cities on sale? Funnily enough - despite the fact that early settlers showed very little imagination when it came to naming towns and villages, which is why there is a Newcastle (in New South Wales), a York (in Western Australia) and a Sheffield (in Tasmania) - there is nowhere in Australia called Manchester other than in department stores. Because Manchester in Australian means the department where you can locate sheets, linen and towels.

How I have been married to an Australian for 18 years and not discovered this I do not know. Maybe it is because he and I have never, in 18 years of marriage, been shopping together for sheets and towels in Australia - or any other country. Men don't usually get it with sheets or towels, do they? How many men do you know who understand the importance of threadcount? Not needing any sheets or towels, I stuck to the handbag shopping with my sister-in-law. I probably don't need any new handbags either, but that's not the point. When you are living 24 hours a day with four males who just need inhale food and generate laundry, retail therapy offers an escape. However, handbag shopping in Melbourne was not easy. I ended up calling Vogue Australia for help and even then, armed with the name and address of Christine, the chicest place to buy handbags in Melbourne, I had great difficulty finding it. That is because it is located in a basement in Flinders Lane with no shop window and almost no sign. If I was stressed coping with my family, it was a lot worse walking up and down Flinders Lane wondering why we couldn't spot a handbag shop. I do not call a business card, in a glass recess to the left of the door, proper signage.

As we descended into a subterranean world with no natural light and red-velvet-lined walls, my sister-in-law remarked that it resembled a brothel. I pointed out that I knew it wasn't one because in Victoria these are legal and so very well signed, and a damn sight easier to find. Fortunately the shop turned out to be worth finding, with serious handbags aplenty including a whole wall dedicated to Anya Hindmarch.

All the stress involved in a family Christmas, a terrible Ashes result and the challenge of finding an incognito handbag shop is putting lines on my face. No matter: on my return to the UK I discovered that Single Girlfriend had bought me, as a Christmas present, 60ml of Crème de la Mer, the very expensive face cream. I am not sure if this is generous or insulting, but it remains unopened as I am not sure how to use it. Neither the instructions nor the jar tell you if it is day or night cream (or both), how much to use or if you need some sun protection as well (what is the SPF of Crème de la Mer, for goodness sake?). Families look easy now that I am stressed about how to use a £130 (2007) jar of moisturiser.

Better the Davos you know

Jan 27, 2007

I have never been to Davos. This is quite an admission from a woman who, some claim, would attend the opening of an envelope if the right people and the right champagne were present. But then Davos is supposed to be a very serious, weighty networking opportunity and maybe I am not serious enough (although I am probably weighty enough). If I wish to be invited to Davos in the future I had better come up with a way to make myself sound more serious and weighty, and spend less time mentioning my personal grooming or handbag purchasing activities.

I am serious and weighty enough to be asked to Davos, I promise. In the meantime, I am only invited to events such as the IFR Bank of the Year Awards. Quick reminder: this is when 1,500 investment bankers, their public relations staff and every journalist they can drum up gather in the presence of HRH the Princess Royal (Princess Anne to you and me) to pat each other on the back and raise a vast sum of money (this year more than £2.3m) for Save the Children. Last year I came within a metre of meeting Anshu Jain, the arrestingly handsome head of markets at Deutsche Bank, so was hoping for an even closer encounter this time.

It was not to be. Anshu Jain did not attend. I was a guest of the Thundering Herd, who sat me next to someone called Henri. Henri was very good company and also very attractive, but happened to be a woman. What is it with women who work for investment banks and gender-bending names? Another very attractive woman I know at an investment bank is called Gavin. And despite both these women having been allocated more than their fair share in the looks department, they are both still single. Is there a message here?

Henri might still be single but she came in very handy when it came to the detailed interpretation of the awards. I used to work in a bank, and consider myself more financially literate than the man in the street, but the abuse of English by the banking industry is so bad that I despair. I struggled in particular with the award given to Lloyds TSB for Best Subordinated Financial Bond. They won this with their catchy "perpetual non-call 10" which they had used last year to raise $1.1bn. Fortunately Henri had been involved in this transaction in some capacity and was able to explain that, far from being perpetual (definition: continuing for ever), this was a bond that could be redeemed (so why call it perpetual?) but only every 10 years - and only then if they wish to. I see.

I am not sure that HRH did, even though she had someone very serious and weighty next to her to help: Lloyd Blankfein, chairman of Goldman Sachs. He is bound to be at Davos, I should think, and if you see him there please ask if he had to explain to the Princess Royal what a perpetual non-call 10 was. Of course, she might not have asked, although she did look a little puzzled for most of the evening. Before he rushed off to catch the plane that was waiting for him, Lloyd may have also been asked what a "dual- tranche" was or why Bradford & Bingley, a UK mortgage lender, had needed one to borrow 550m Swiss francs. Maybe, with all the climate change going on, UK citizens are rushing to buy in the Alps to ensure a white Christmas. Or perhaps they have so many serious and weighty people to take to Davos that they need a few Swiss francs to pay for it. The Xstrata £1.3bn Accelerated Bookbuild might have interested the royal mind, or perhaps, in my view, the most nonsensical award category - the leveraged loan. What is a loan if it is not leveraged? Please. TDC won this category with an €211.75bn transaction, which I suggest should simply be called a loan.

Last year this function was noteworthy for two reasons unconnected with Anshu Jain. One was that the ex-boyfriend I glimpse once a year was at the back of the room on an insignificant table. I am pleased to report that this year he was on table 107. The back of the room is the most appropriate place for someone who lacked the good taste to marry me when he could.

The other reason last year was worth noting is that I went home with a souvenir: the table centrepiece, a vase engraved with the event and date and so useless after that night. Next day the "engraving" turned out to be a sticker, so the verb "to souvenir" was elevated to the verb "to steal". This year they had placed engraved candles inside vases, so I souvenired a candle. Souveniring is another bad use of English and inappropriate for a serious and weighty professional woman. And probably why I have not been invited to Davos.

Warm invitations

Feb 03, 2007

Climate change remains high on everyone's agenda and was the subject of an official session at Davos, the World Economic Forum's annual meeting, this year. Looking at the Davos programme, I'm afraid I found myself stifling a yawn. I just can't get excited about the future of the dollar, housing deflation or frozen trade talks. They even had a session called "Why do brains sleep?" led by Professor Lord Robert Winston. I felt like writing to him and suggesting that mine is inclined to sleep when reading Davos session lists.

This is neither the affected indifference of the non-participant, nor the result of reading the schedule before 7am. Rather, I realise I am a narrow-minded, middle-aged mother-of-three who has never really had more than a passing interest in macroeconomics.

I was last entreated to take an interest in the subject at the London Business School 18 years ago, where I was taught by Lord Currie of Marylebone, now the chairman of Ofcom, who was then plain Professor David Currie. I don't remember being very interested in it then either, and suspect I turned up in class simply to admire his lovely brown eyes.

Eighteen years ago, the World Economic Forum was debating different matters, but then, 18 years ago my garden wasn't blooming in January. There is no doubt that we are experiencing climate change; but is there really any proof that human beings are to blame? As the last ice age came to an end, I am sure the mammoths didn't gather on a mountain in Switzerland worrying that it was their fault. It was going to happen whatever they did. I suspect the same is true now, but hey, some snow, a few drinks parties and a lot of networking are good for most people.

All that said, the mere mention of flowers and networking has focused my mind on this year's Chelsea Flower Show. The gala preview is on the evening of Monday May 21 and I have already booked the hairdresser. For those of you reading this column in places like Seattle and Shanghai rather than Surbiton or Sunderland, the Chelsea gala preview is the hottest ticket in town for anyone who is anyone in the goldfish bowl of the UK capital markets. Unlike Davos, where you can join in by shelling out €222,000 and sending along your CEO on a private jet, this is an invitation-only event.

One can see the attractions of a Swiss mountain resort, but what gets all those CEOs into a tent in the grounds of a retirement home for former military personnel? The displays of rose bushes and award-winning garden designs? The knowledge that Her Majesty the Queen has walked around a few hours before? No, it is quite simple. The reason that almost all of them turn up is that the investment banks that host them have the foresight to invite their wives too. Which CEO in his right mind is going to tell his wife that he turned down an invitation to the gala preview of the Chelsea Flower Show?

Climate change may force the show to be held earlier in the future, and I thought for a moment that this had already happened last week, when I was at a social gathering at London's Victoria and Albert Museum.

It had all the hallmarks of Chelsea and I had a strong sense of déjà vu; present were chairmen and CEOs responsible for 75 per cent of the capitalisation of the FTSE 100, plus leading investment bankers, all drinking champagne and eating canapes. I also had the same problem as at the flower show last year - I only got to speak to a tenth of the people I'd have liked to, and yet again missed Lord Stevenson of Coddenham. But this wasn't May - it was mid- January.

And it wasn't the flower show, of course. It was a party given by Sir Win Bischoff, Robert Swannell and David Challen of Citigroup to celebrate a combined 100 years of working together. It so closely resembled the flower show (apart from the lack of flowers) that I could have sworn I was in SW3 rather than SW7.

The other big difference was the almost total lack of wives. There were some (including those of our hosts) but for some reason (presumably lack of flowers) very few spouses had chosen to accompany their loved ones to a cocktail party in South Kensington on a Tuesday night. I have to say that this made networking 100 per cent easier than at Chelsea, since one didn't have to conduct polite conversations about flowers and children before launching into the likely prospect of significant M&A activity in the banking sector in 2007.

It was a stellar guest list which our hosts helpfully printed and handed out, and which most of us consulted when we got home to see who we'd missed. No matter, I will catch them on May 21, after the hairdresser and the beauty therapist and wearing a new Diane von Furstenberg dress, because you can't be seen in the same one twice. And hopefully I will then (as I did last week) end the night on the dance floor at Annabel's rather than discussing frozen trade talks.

Risky business

Feb 10, 2007

I have not drunk any alcohol for a month, not even a glass of Krug. No, I have not been detoxing, nor am I on medication. First, I gave up for a week, because someone I knew had done so and I wanted to see if I could too. Then it became a challenge to see if I could manage a second week. Finally, I discovered I had lost weight. So I have stuck with it.

I am not going to look like Kate Moss any time soon, but it does prove that I was consuming a lot of calories via a wine glass. Early in January I went to a shoot in Shropshire and faced my first real test. At dinner, in the company of seven men, it was easy - I just drank fizzy water and told them I was pregnant. Half of them laughed and the rest didn't know whether to take me seriously or not. Quite why a lot of middle-aged men running financial services companies thought it so unlikely that I was still capable of procreation, I do not know. When I do become menopausal, I shall probably be very fed up, but I have to say it looks appealing. I would quite like a month when I didn't get spots suddenly for no good reason and then start yelling at the Cost Centres. (On reflection, I yell at the Cost Centres all month long if they won't unload the dishwasher or make their beds when required.)

I never, of course, yell at anyone in the office. In particular, I never yell at the Lovely Lucinda, even when she went to Dubai on holiday and then the threatened British Airways strike looked likely to keep her there. She sent a text message helpfully suggesting that I might like to outsource her to Dubai. No, LL, I would not. I need you back. Apart from anything else, you are the company's designated health and safety officer and if you don't come back I will have to find someone else. Besides, the light bulb on the top landing has blown.

I might feel healthy from not drinking, but I am not sure how safe I feel. Health and safety is something they never tell you about at business school and you might not learn that if you have more than five employees, you have to do a full risk assessment and keep a poster prominently displayed in the workplace. Fortunately the government has published an introduction to health and safety for small businesses (http://www.hse.gov.uk/smallbusinesses/ gettingstarted.htm), so I have learnt how many people die (60) and are injured (4,000) from falls at work. Apparently one of the main causes is ladders. Perhaps, LL, you had better forget the lightbulb.

I know all this because I have just had to sign our health and safety policy. This has got me worrying about the office trampoline. It's not a full-size model, and not even company property - one of our team asked if she could install it for her lunchtime exercise routine each day. We have put it in the room with a television so she can watch the soaps while getting rid of the calories. I have even been known to use it myself on mornings when it is too cold or too wet to go for a run.

As well as not drinking, I am trying to look after myself better in 2007. So is Cost Centre #1, who has taken up squash in response to the "10-point Wellness Plan" his headmaster has sent all pupils and their parents. The letter exhorts us to eat more pheasant because.the selenium is good for you. Well, no problem there in the Moneypenny household. But having read it, I decided it looks very much like a health and safety policy - mostly common sense.

CC#1 wrote a review of the Wellness Plan for the school newspaper, in which he failed to mention the pheasant recommendation but did observe that the encouragement to refrain from brief and meaningless sexual fulfilment might go unheeded in a school full of teenage boys.

The trampoline may use up the calories, but I have doubts on health and safety grounds. What is our liability if someone bounces off and breaks their leg? Should all bouncing staff, myself included, sign a disclaimer? Should I get rid of it altogether? I also use my skipping rope in the hall, do press-ups, and run up and down the stairs for exercise. Are all these banned on health and safety grounds? I would consult my health and safety officer, but as I write she is still on holiday in Dubai, where I am not sure what methods she has employed to keep off the calories.

In her absence, the latest alarming piece of paper to appear is not a health and safety poster but a brochure from Starbucks detailing the calories in their products. Did you know that a skimmed milk, grande white chocolate mocha - my favourite drink - has 441 calories? A glass of wine, of course, has only 80. Maybe a month off the coffee comes next.

Too late to be a petal pusher

Feb 17, 2007

How far ahead is your diary booked? My furthest forward commitment other than Christmas Day, which I have promised to spend at home, is October 19. People such as the Queen and public company directors run a forward calendar of at least 18 months, which makes my date to shoot game in Scotland in October seem almost last- minute.

On January 29, I invited the finance director of a very large public company to accompany me to the Chelsea Flower Show gala preview on the evening of Monday May 21. She was unable to accept my invitation, not because she doesn't like flowers or will be out of the country that evening, but because she had already agreed to go with someone else.

I am sure I would have been a more interesting companion, but no matter. My mistake, it turns out, was not to have asked early enough. Personally I would have thought that four months' notice for a couple of hours early on a Monday evening in May was plenty, but apparently not. Since accepting her original invitation, she has had seven more. So not only was I not early enough, I was positively tardy.

I consulted another finance director - of an equally large public company. Had he already been invited? Yes, and he had accepted the first invitation he got. It was not from a very exciting host but, he told me, he had learnt his lesson the hard way. Last year, he turned down the first invitation he received in the hope that someone more interesting would ask him. This is classic game theory behaviour, as my colleague Tim Harford, the Undercover Economist, will tell you, but it didn't serve him well. No-one else asked him, and game theory has no strategies for coping with your wife when she discovers at a late stage that she will not be attending the Chelsea Flower Show gala preview.

From a host's perspective, the lesson to be learned is that the more boring you are, the sooner you need to get your invitations out. No wonder the big four accountancy firms get theirs out over Christmas to be first on their clients' desks when they return in the new year. My company now faces a dilemma. Should we invite some B-list (or at this late stage, probably C-list) company directors, or give up on the idea of inviting anyone from outside and just take ourselves? I have decided on the latter: we will be well represented at the event, and with no guests of our own we can go round and chat to those who accepted invitations from boring hosts and long to escape.

One event I shall not be attending in May is the wedding of my American Girlfriend. She is marrying a banker a few years older than herself, who I know because he was a reader of my column for many years. Once, long before he met AG, he wrote and invited me out to dinner. I accepted on the understanding that it was somewhere low key. We dined at a pizzeria in Chelsea and I was vain enough not to want to use my spectacles to see the menu. Holding the laminated card at arm's length, I suddenly noticed that smoke was rising from behind the list of pizzas. This was swiftly followed by an overwhelming smell of melting plastic. It was at that moment that I realised the menu had been set alight by the table candle. My attempt to look super-cool with no glasses had resulted in my looking super-stupid and accident-prone.

But it was not this incident that led to my omission from their guest list. It is, the bride tells me, because they are trying "to minimise the carbon footprint" of their wedding. Now, I can forgive AG many things, including the fact that she comes from California and does yoga, but I am worried that she is taking all this new age stuff a bit far. As she furnished further details, I became even more concerned. She is, she tells me, tying the knot in a "peace barn" (yes, really) overlooking the ocean in California. I did recover my composure a bit when she said she was going to wear a Vera Wang dress, but lost it again when she explained that she was hoping to go barefoot. The knockout blow came when she told me of her plans for a carbon-minimising blessing to take place in the UK in June, when the newly-weds will be blessed by her healer. Her healer! Why not her acupuncturist as well for good measure?

I am definitely boring. I got married in church with shoes on, for goodness' sake. No wonder I have to get my Chelsea gala preview invitations out earlier.

Form and function

Mar 03, 2007

What makes you anxious? In my opinion anxiety, like regret, is an overrated emotion. I am convinced that it does nothing for my wellbeing and might even aggravate the ageing process, which at 44 is an important consideration for me. The most anxious I have been recently was during a return flight from New York after having had to pack a jar of Crème de la Mer in my checked luggage. My jewellery stays in my hand luggage, but al-Qaeda has ensured that I must risk putting a £130 jar of face cream in the hold.

I still don't know how to use it properly. Despite complaining about the paucity of instructions on the packaging a few weeks back, no one has e-mailed to enlighten me. Indeed, one reader got in touch to ask that were I to find out, would I share the information with her? Where are the people at Estée Lauder? Do none of you read the *FT* at the weekend? If Sir Nicholas Goodison can write in to commend me for having read his meteorology masterpiece (*English Barometers*, 1680-1860, second edition) then surely someone from 767 Fifth Avenue could get in touch?

Meanwhile Cost Centre #1, who accompanied me on the plane, was anxious about something else. He was convinced that a group of young men on the flight were members of a rock band, but could not work out which one. I dispensed with dinner, as I usually do on overnight transatlantic flights to maximise sleeping time, and utilised the flat bed to full effect, but next to me CC#1 remained awake, eating, watching movies and fretting about the band. For the first time, I regretted that Silverjet only has one class - business. If we'd been on BA my son would have been consigned to economy and wouldn't even have spotted the rock band. *(Silverjet sadly ceased trading in 2008)*

I needed my beauty sleep because (a) my Crème de la Mer was out of reach and (b) the next day I was due to go to dinner at a girlfriend's house. I had a brief anxious moment after she told me that she and her guests planned to change for dinner.

Change for dinner? On a Saturday night in Gloucestershire? Don't worry, she said, it's not black tie. I should hope not. What is the dress code then, I asked. "Country smart," she replied.

What on earth is country smart, I wondered? As I turned up in my shooting dinner kit - black evening trousers, red velvet jacket and statutory cleavage - I discovered that I was not the only one to have been puzzled. Another guest's stylish French wife - wearing black trousers, ankle boots, a beaded cardigan and a lovely complexion that had clearly benefited from more Crème de la Mer (or similar) than mine - took one look at me and berated her husband for not having briefed her properly on our hostess's dress requirements.

There was worse to come. At dinner, my girlfriend, who is getting married later in the year, disclosed her wedding plans. The ceremony will take place in church (good), she plans to wear shoes (even better) and the dress code will be morning suits (fine - Mr M has two, one for fat days and another, which admittedly has not had much use, for thinner days). But the dance in the evening will be - wait for it - white tie. What does "white tie" mean? asked my Gallic dining companion. "You'll need to get the tiara out of the bank," said her husband. She can clearly afford Crème de la Mer.

I am now very anxious. I have one friend getting blessed by her healer when she marries and now another expecting me to turn up dressed for the Duchess of Richmond's ball in Brussels on the eve of Waterloo. What is it with these women who are entering into marriage for the first time later in life? My white-tie friend is two months younger than me, so will be 45 when she ties the knot. The problem is that she has had far too long to think about what she wants by way of a wedding. Or she has been watching too many films set in 19th-century Europe.

By the time that CC#1 had watched several films set in 21st-century America he still couldn't work out the name of the band and went to sleep, only to start fretting about it again at the baggage carousel at Luton. My suitcase - and contents - appeared safely and I found myself in the revolving door leaving the terminal with one of the band, whose attire was rather more urban cool than country smart. Of course I asked him the name of his band. *The Kings of Leon*, was the reply. I relayed this to CC#1 and asked if it would have made him any less anxious on the flight had he known. "You're kidding," he said. "I wouldn't have slept a wink - I'd have been too excited."

I have never heard of the *Kings of Leon*, so I can't comment. I can comment, though, on how infuriating it is to possess an expensive jar of face cream that I don't know how to use. Estée Lauder is holding an investor day on Tuesday, March 6. If you happen to be going, please ask them to send me some instructions? It will save me a lot of anxiety.

What's the use?

Mar 10, 2007

Charles Darwin died in April 1882, almost exactly 80 years before I was born. I had to look that fact up, but my interest in the man is not a superficial one. (Although I might add that I have stayed, during the Hay Festival, in a bed and breakfast run by one of his direct descendants - see www.churchhousekington.co.uk for a totally different approach to self-promotion.) I fully subscribe to Darwin's theory of natural selection - the survival of the fittest.

Which is why, more mornings a week than I care for, I am to be found kicking and punching my way through an hour of exercise. At least one of those mornings will be under the supervision of Holly the Sadist at the gym in the Royal Automobile Club. For those of you reading this outside the UK (and I know this column is read by Canadians in Spain as well as, no doubt, Spaniards in Canada) the RAC is a traditional gentlemen's club in Pall Mall that has latterly accepted lady members and is so posh it can't bring itself to set up lanes in the swimming pool.

HTS is a great personal trainer, and a demanding boxing coach, but even she has her limitations. Emerging dripping from the pool last Tuesday ahead of a black-tie event, I realised that I had left my underarm razor at home. I wrapped a towel around me and went to seek emergency supplies. HTS offered to investigate and was told that the RAC has a large supply of disposable razors - in the men's changing room. She refused to go in there, even in the noble cause of my armpits. (Yes, I do wax almost everything you can see, and a lot that you can't, but that's one part of me to which I still take a razor.) Why does the men's changing room have a monopoly on complimentary disposable razors? Why are they not in the ladies' changing room as well? I think this is a blatant case of sex discrimination. Women have just as much unwanted hair, I promise you.

But hirsute or not, I am getting fitter, so I should survive. Overweight, middle-aged mothers of three are not yet on the Red List, the official register published by the Conservation Union that shows which species are becoming endangered. I am not sure why we need lists of endangered species. If species are not fit enough to survive, then surely they should be allowed to become extinct?

The Red List (www.iucnredlist.org) evaluates thousands of species and assigns them a category according to how close they are to extinction. For example, it has evaluated 87 varieties of parakeet.

Now, I know this is going to cause my in-tray to overflow, but I have to ask - what is the point of a parakeet? Should it matter to us whether cyanoramphus malherbi or psittacula eques becomes extinct or not? What would Darwin's view have been of the Red List's assertion that the former have suffered a "population crash" because of "rat invasions" between 1990 and 2000? I suspect he might have said that, if the parakeets couldn't fend off the rats, then they shouldn't be around to tell the story.

I am told by people who study this kind of thing at university that endangered species have a "preservation value". This is made up of their "option value" (what we are prepared to pay to still have the use of a parakeet in the future, just in case we ever think of a use), their "bequest value" (what we may be prepared to pay to be able to pass the possible future use of a parakeet on to the next generation - I am not sure that the Cost Centres could come up with a use either), and their "existence value". Existence value? What is that? Apparently it is that which we might be prepared to pay to keep a species in existence even if no use is contemplated. Forget parakeets - what is the existence value of husbands, I wonder?

Back home in South Oxfordshire, a part of the world where most of the population has never seen a parakeet, let alone thought of a use for one, I spend part of every weekend at the South Moreton Boxing Club. This is a relatively new club, not even a year old, but it looks likely to survive and is putting on its first big event, a white-collar evening, on March 31, in the unlikely metropolis of Wallingford, an Oxfordshire market town. Here we really will see the survival of the fittest as 20 club members, from policemen to lawyers, engineers to farmers, battle it out without a parakeet in sight.

I have no idea whether I will be attending, as that weekend should see the return of a species you would be forgiven for having thought already extinct - the Moneypenny dog, still away at gun dog boarding school. Mr M will be able to resume his fitness regime of walking her every day before breakfast, and I can start work on getting her used to my voice commands before the onset of the next shooting season. At which time I shall be shooting not parakeets, but pheasants, birds that even Charles Darwin could have seen a use for.

In the shadow of greatness

Apr 07, 2007

The City of London is the ultimate bastion of communism. That was the view expressed by Anthony Hilton, veteran financial commentator, at a breakfast I attended the other day. The reason? Workers, rather than the owners of capital, command the biggest share of the profits. He was referring to the gargantuan bonuses distributed across the investment banking industry in the Square Mile, but it could equally apply to Wall Street. In what other industry do shareholders patiently stand by, accepting scraps from the table, while profits are looted by the staff?

No wonder competition to secure a job in investment banking is so intense. It's not enough to be graduating from Oxford or Cambridge with a first class degree and to speak four languages. I am told by several banks that one of the ways they whittle down thousands of applicants to the 200-300 that they interview each year is by looking for relevant work experience, or internships.

Proper internships are paid (or unpaid) temporary positions in companies, taken up by young people still in education. These are best done in large companies that can spare the time and resources needed to invest in the intern and which intend to benefit from a decent length of service from them. There is no tradition of internships in the UK. Instead, by the time I left university I had had several jobs, starting at 15 washing up in a pub. One summer was spent at Gatwick airport in a bright red uniform ushering drunken passengers on to charter planes, but it is hard to see how that prepared me for a career in capital markets. Equally, working in a ski resort taught me how to feed 20 people on £10 a day, but that was not a skill that I needed in the City.

In the US and continental Europe, by contrast, the tradition of the intern is well established. Students apply to competitive schemes and spend their summer holidays working to improve their job prospects. Many of them will do several internships. Young people in the Netherlands and Germany in particular seem to be in danger of becoming grandparents before they get an undergraduate degree as they procrastinate through endless internships.

In the UK, we have our own way of doing things. The term "work experience" is one I dread hearing. Work experience is when someone asks to foist their 16-year-old child on to you for a week or two so that he or she can get an idea of their career options. Some schools even make it part of their syllabus. Last summer my company agreed to take on two such young people, for the usual appalling reason that their parents were well known to us and therefore had undue influence. This took up a massive amount of time, not least because their schools sent inspectors to check out our offices and our adherence to health and safety rules.

The girls themselves were delightful, but that isn't the point. Would we have taken them on were they not the children of people we knew? Of course not. The exercise took up valuable resources with no obvious gain to our business other than two sets of hugely grateful parents. And of course, this system isn't limited to school-age children. We are also often asked to create holiday jobs for undergraduates and even "starter" jobs for graduates, many of whom seem, to my horror, not to know what they want to do in life.

I must admit that I too use this system. Cost Centre #1 is 17 and will be applying to university this year. His CV will list several work experience stints at various big companies. But I wish there were a different way to help our children start their careers.

As a reasonably solvent parent, I would even be prepared to pay to get CC#1 the relevant work experience he needs. I know that there will be those up in arms about this idea, that it would favour the rich over the poor. But how is it different from his experience so far? I have paid for his education, so why not pay for work experience too? If you are going to give a child an advantage, why not go all the way? Surely that is better than begging favours?

I have decided to start a company that exists purely to deliver work experience to undecided graduates. I plan to staff it with new graduates who need both career advice and a starter job. We will limit their contracts to three months, long enough to get something sensible on to their CV and to be able to give them a reference. And we will charge their parents for taking them on. Capitalism at its worst? Yes. But it is only an extension of what goes on already. And who knows, a few of our "interns" might even make it into the Square Mile, where they too can embrace communism by looting shareholder returns by way of bonuses. They will earn enough to send their children to private school - and so begins the cycle all over again.

Windsors and losers

Apr 14, 2007

Last week I underwent a health procedure. I shall not spell out in detail the exact nature of the event as I don't want to spoil your weekend, but suffice to say that it involved warm water and mirrors. Why did I do this? It took an hour out of the working day, left me feeling rather nauseated and the subsequent detoxification effects gave me a headache and brought me out in spots. Plus it cost £70. But I was instructed to go by my youthful and energetic personal trainer, Holly the Sadist, who assured me that it would be the key to a healthier life.

She sent me to someone to whom she goes herself, a lady I suspect is almost as old as my mother. Why her? HTS explained that she used to go elsewhere and then someone she knew recommended this particular practitioner. She followed up on the recommendation not because of the professional reputation of the service, nor the lady's gentle technique (both of which I can attest to). Instead, it was because the woman's clients included the late Diana, Princess of Wales. That, HTS tells me, was enough to make her book an appointment immediately. Ten years after her death, why should Diana's choice of any service or item make a difference to whether you, me or HTS want to purchase or use it?

In the UK we like our royal endorsements. If a company is used regularly by a member of the royal household it may be granted a "royal warrant", which allows it to display the coat of arms of the approving royal and the inscription "by appointment". There are more than 1,000 companies with a royal warrant, and choosing to use a supplier selected by the Queen might give some people comfort. Fortunately, there exists a website dedicated to listing the contact details of all the companies so honoured, www.royalwarrant.org.

Any information that speeds up decision-making is welcome to me, so, fresh from the nauseating health procedure, I went to the website to discover what other services I might use. You can search the site by category, so I started with pest control.

In our old offices we had a rodent problem for a while, despite being on the third floor, and in the end we called in a large and well-known company to sort out the problem. We wasted time getting a quote and then thinking about it. And when we did eventually hire them, they didn't do a brilliant job and we had to have them back a few more times. Why did we bother? Why did we not follow HM the Queen and get Rokill to dispose of our mice? I notice that she has a separate supplier for mole catching. We have not had a mouse problem in our new offices, and I can't recall the appearance of a mole, but it is good to know that if we do, I shall know where to go.

And why stop at rodents and burrowing mammals? Her Majesty seems to face many of the same decisions as us. Choosing office furniture, for example. When we moved offices, we had to purchase new office equipment. This took the most ridiculous amount of time. First, I had to consult about 10 catalogues and discuss them with our fitting-out contractor. As I was pressed for time, I arranged for him to meet me at the hairdresser, and we considered the pros and cons of various products while my highlights were being done. Then, having narrowed it down to three potential suppliers, my office manager and I spent a whole morning touring furniture showrooms in London while considering such mind-numbing details as central processing unit storage and cabling. Why didn't I go straight to one of the companies used by HM?

Finally, the vexed issue of mobile phones. We provide telephones and BlackBerries to all our staff, who now number more than 20 people. Her Majesty employs rather more than 20 people, but not for her the confusing array of tariffs and hardware facing the weary procurement officer. No, she goes to The Carphone Warehouse. And until I called and pointed it out, Charles Dunstone's personal e-mail address was listed under their entry on the royal warrant site. I haven't been privy to their correspondence, but one can imagine it. "My dear Charles, I was thinking about issuing the new Nokia N95 to my under-butler and wondered whether you would recommend the pay-as-you-go or the monthly tariff? And while we are at it,

Prince Philip is not managing his BlackBerry very well since his new one doesn't have a Qwerty keyboard and he is not very good at predictive texting. Do you have any suggestions? Yours sincerely, HM Queen Elizabeth II."

Charles Dunstone is a busy man. He employs many more than 20 people - 20,000 across the group to be precise - and no doubt works as many hours of the day as I do. I wonder whether he also has a personal trainer and undertakes health procedures using warm water and mirrors. Perhaps he could publish a list of the suppliers he has personally chosen so that people like me can take advantage of his recommendations?

Adventures in Bodenland

Apr 21, 2007

Some habits are hard to break. Writing this column to its set length, for example. Since October 1999, when Cost Centre #1 had still not celebrated his 10th birthday and CC#3 was not yet walking or talking, I have written this column to a length of between 800 and 900 words.

Admittedly, it had a couple of years in another publication along the way, and in 2005 even a year off, when I turned my attention to other things. But even so, I have written more than 300 Mrs M columns to that length, which is understandably habit-forming.

Now, with CC#1 in his 18th year, I am about to have to change my ways. From next weekend my column is being "revamped" and I am to deliver only 700 words. This is not because the powers that be have found me too frothy (you can just imagine the meeting - "please can we have less of the personal grooming and more on international trade talks?") but because fewer words looks nicer on the page. So I shall have to acquire a new habit: writing less.

CC#3 (now eight) is able to walk, talk and use bad language. In an altercation with one of his brothers over a football during Easter weekend, he called him an idiot. This alone was enough to get a reprimand, but he preceded the word idiot with an adjective that I will not repeat. I am so deaf these days that I did not hear him, but from the speed at which his father raced off to admonish him and from the length of his subsequent banishment, in disgrace, I knew that he must have said something totally unacceptable. This is one habit he'd better abandon before he takes it up.

Our Easter holiday has become something of a habit. For the past few years my whole family (my parents, two sisters and latterly my married sister's spouse and twin sons) have spent Easter at the Priory Bay Hotel on the Isle of Wight. It is one of those rare places that works whether you are eight, 18, 48 or 80, and you can even take your family pet, so my parents' dog comes too.

You are able, if you wish, to give your children high tea at 5.30pm, and eat later in a child-free environment. Alternatively, there is a separate dining room for those extraordinary people who wish to dine with their small cost centres at a time when I consider that they should be in bed. This child-friendliness means the hotel attracts many families and provides unlimited playmates for CCs#1, 2 and 3. It does however mean that you step into "Bodenland" for the weekend.

Boden sells by direct mail and has become the preferred clothing of the upwardly mobile British middle class and, in particular, stay- at-home mothers (whom I assume have the time necessary to read the catalogue and go on to the internet and buy all those pastel coloured sweatshirts). The catalogues make all the families depicted look impossibly content and nothing like ours, where eight-year-olds swear at their brothers.

The wine list at the Priory Bay puzzled me this year even more than the question of where CC#3 is learning such bad language. Three of the wines, all from South Africa, are highlighted in red and the footnote says "recommended by Andrew Palmer". I wonder what first- time visitors to the hotel make of this. It is hardly as if the footnote reads "recommended by Jancis Robinson". Who is Mr Palmer? Why should his recommendation matter?

Now, I know who Andrew Palmer is. He founded the New

Covent Garden Soup Company, sold it and then spent the proceeds (or some of them) on buying the Priory Bay and turning it into a luxury hotel for people wearing Boden, but that information is not readily available in the hotel. Unless you ask, the closest you are likely to get is to notice on the headed paper that the hotel is owned by a company called Peartime Limited whose directors are RA Palmer and JS Palmer. Further investigation, if you can be bothered, will tell you that Andrew's first name is Rowland. Quite what qualifies Mr Palmer to pronounce on wine I don't know. I asked our waiter. "He knows a lot about wine," I was told.

Well, Mr M knows a lot about wine as well. He arrived at the Priory Bay straight from a week in Bordeaux at the annual trade tastings, where he sampled more than 400 wines from the 2006 vintage. After living alone in a hotel room for that time, he had acquired the irritating habit of leaving the loo seat up, and did so four times during the first two days of our holiday. A habit that I find particularly irritating, and one that I had to break for him by the end of the weekend.

It's not all hot air

Apr 28, 2007

I grew up in the 1960s and 1970s when the UN Security Council was preoccupied with the nuclear arms race, the campaign for nuclear disarmament was at its peak and women with unshaven armpits were protesting outside the US airbase at Greenham Common in Berkshire.

I had mixed views on this at the time. While I felt that nuclear disarmament was probably a good thing - if rather impractical - I just couldn't understand the hairy armpits, having shaved mine religiously since I was a teenager.

For a while, world peace was all that young things in Islington talked about at dinner parties, and you could even do degrees in it at university.

Thirty years later, the environment is our new zeitgeist-y cause. Green issues are the subject of dinner-party chatter for north Londoners, and plenty of institutions offer degrees in environmental subjects.

We in the older generation seem to fall into three camps in the face of unrelenting debate about whether polar bears are in danger of extinction or whether the UK should legislate on light bulbs. Some people simply deny that climate change is happening.

I think we can dismiss this, as all the statistics show that it is happening and even the most diehard ostrich has had to get its head out of the sand on the subject. Climate change is upon us, whether we like it or not.

The second camp is the "it is happening, but it is not our fault" category. This view has less evidence to support it, but it does have some backers, although judging by my postbag the last time that I ventured forth on this subject, it seems to be considered heresy to say so.

The third category could be summarised as "it is happening, and it is our fault, but it's not worth doing anything about it because China and India are polluting the world so badly that someone who installs solar panels on their house in Wolverhampton or switches to energy-efficient light bulbs in Des Moines, Iowa, is not going to make any difference."

This last argument is almost certainly true, just as surely as it was true back in the 1970s that a few women with unshaven armpits were not going to stop the world's nuclear arms race. However, not doing something just because China is not doing it strikes me as a very unsound decision. On that basis we might question whether we should bother with democracy, freedom of the press, or even the manufacture and consumption of Cheddar cheese - none of which is popular in China.

Perhaps remarkably, I find myself having more and more green tendencies. At our office we employ an events manager who also happens to have a degree in recycling (OK, correct term "environmental management"), though she doesn't (yet) live in Islington.

She is helping me with my latest attempt to green the office - ordering some recycled stationery.

In particular, I am keen that our office pencils should be recycled in some way.

I had thought this request would yield a reasonably small selection, but no. Choosing right-on pencils is almost as confusing as ordering a cup of coffee in the US. You can order pencils made from plastic cups, CD cases, paper, car parts, recycled milk bottles and computer cases. Then you can get them made from old newspapers, sustainable timber, scraps of denim and even from plastic lunch trays.

Moving on to pens, some are made from corn starch, which feels like plastic but will dissolve in landfill within three months. All of these are from suppliers in the UK - I wonder how many more inventive products I would find in the US?

The pencils I like most are made from recycled money. I love the notion of recycling cash and reminding our staff that money needs to work for a living, just like every other factor of production.

I used to think that I was somewhat set in my ways, too old to change my mind about things and not keen enough to embrace change. But I am changing the pencils, and who knows what else may follow. I still intend, though, to continue to shave my armpits. Maybe someone will invent a recycled razor?

Fees release me, let me go

May 05, 2007

Expenditure on the Cost Centres escalates daily. It is not just the fees, I remind myself as I organise payments to three different schools. (The current annual total is £60,000 - out of taxed income - so we are in effect paying twice.) No, for the 18 weeks a year that the Cost Centres are on holiday we also have to feed and clothe them, as well as pay for their social life.

Then there are the incentive payments. CC#1 has only once met his targets, which are set by me at the start of every term or examination cycle. That was when he produced a string of As in his common entrance examinations and was awarded a state-of-the-art laptop with vast quantities of memory to run computer games. Subsequent hardware purchases (iPod, video camera, bass guitar, bass guitar amp and so on) have been in lieu of birthday parties. The thought of a bunch of teenagers in the house or even in a tent in the garden is just too terrible to contemplate, so I bribe him out of parties on every occasion.

Over the past three terms, CC#2 has been on a rolling incentive plan for a Sony PS3, a games machine that costs far too much (more than £400) to be attached to only one target. Sadly for our bank balance, he produced the requisite grades and class position three times in a row and so we had to get down to Argos sharpish.

Perhaps I should set more stretching targets, or better still none at all, although it may be too late for that tactic. CC#3, aged eight, suddenly realised this week that despite a much improved report last term and various sporting achievements in football and cricket during the holidays, he was not receiving anything more than his parents' approval. He demanded to know why. I had thought him too young, but the success of his brothers on the risk/reward ratio seems to have permeated. He was bought a game costing £14, a suitable budget given how much the tooth fairy has been forking out lately.

I am not alone in setting targets. For the first time, the Governor of the Bank of England has had to write to the Chancellor of the Exchequer explaining why UK inflation was out of hand at 3.1 per cent when the target was 2 per cent. With private school fee inflation running at between 5 and 8 per cent, Gordon Brown would have received the letter much sooner if school fees were included in the calculations. But that is nothing compared with the spiralling cost of CC#1's mobile telephone bills.

I am in despair about this outlay, which has got worse since he has had a girlfriend. The simple answer - not to ditch the girlfriend, but to switch him to pay-as-you-go - is not my preferred course, because he will simply abandon his phone when it runs out of credit and I won't be able to reach him. Most of the bill, unsurprisingly, is for text messages. Why is it necessary to send so many? "You have to reply if someone texts you - it's rude not to," he replies. It might be polite, but it is also ruinous.

I have appealed to Vodafone, his current supplier, to suggest a solution, and have been canvassing other parents on how they manage. One tells me that T-Mobile has a system that checks with her when her child crosses a pre-set limit and she can then authorise continued credit - or not. I guess her decision depends how many targets her CC has met that month.

My Cleverest Girlfriend, whose only CC has just passed her first birthday, can see all the pitfalls ahead. She is publishing a book this coming week called *Love is Not Enough: A Smart Woman's Guide to Making (and Keeping) Money*.

It's a very useful read, and includes sections on school fees and mobile phones, but I take issue with one statement. "Buying a handbag," declares CG, "is not an emotional experience." But it is! I find it a deeply emotional experience, and one to which I treat myself every year. As an incentive payment for having managed a further 12 months with three children in private schools without going bankrupt.

Read my lips

May 12, 2007

At a meaty 436 pages, Gordon Brown's book - *Speeches 1997-2006* - may not be everyone's idea of light reading, but it is beside the Moneypenny bed at the moment and I am trying to get though a speech every couple of days or so. As we are to have a new prime minister soon, I thought I would mug up on what Brown thinks about life and the universe.

I have devoured books since childhood and continue my education by reading as much, and as widely, as I can. Many people have suggested to me that joining a book group would be a natural way for me to share my newfound knowledge with a select group of others. The problem is that I struggle to see the point of these groups.

It's true that book clubs are proliferating and are particularly popular with women. It has been suggested that some 50,000 clubs might exist in the UK, a figure that alarms me, not least because it is probably an underestimate. But I just don't get why book clubs exist, so I asked my Most Stylish Employee, who is a member of one, to explain.

MSE tells me that hers has only four members. They meet once a month, discuss the book for half an hour at most, and then catch up on all the gossip and work out who should be marrying whom, while drinking copious quantities of alcohol. I wonder why? They could do that in a wine bar without having to go to all the bother of reading a book in advance.

My Most Glamorous Girlfriend is a member of a book club in a London suburb. It is almost exclusively populated with stay-at-home mothers who previously had very demanding and senior jobs, and for whom the book club is an opportunity to get a babysitter for the evening and talk like a grown up for a change. Now, I have a lot of respect for women who give up their careers to take care of their children, because I know what a thankless and exhausting a task it is most of the time, and how the company of toddlers and other stay-at-home mothers can make your brain atrophy. Why do you think I go out to work? So I am not surprised that MGG's fellow members want to exercise their brains once in a while.

But *Genome: The Autobiography of a Species in 23 Chapters* by Matt Ridley? *The God Delusion* by Richard Dawkins? Please. MGG is no slouch - she has an upper second class degree in English literature from Bristol, for goodness' sake - but does she really want to read these books, let alone make notes and then, after a hard day's work and a serious commute, turn up to debate the finer points of difficult subjects? Wouldn't she rather catch an episode of Desperate Housewives with a glass of wine?

Her book club holds an annual planning meeting, when members submit suggestions - in writing - with synopses and notes to support their nomination. What would MGG like to have submitted? *Notting Hell* by Rachel Johnson. However, she knew better than that, and tried to keep with the pace by suggesting Ian Rankin's *The Naming of the Dead* and William

Boyd's *Restless*. Neither was chosen. I suspect they were not highbrow enough for the mothers that mattered.

MGG assures me that she enjoys this and is soldiering on with determination, rather like Gordon Brown. I simply do not understand why. She is about to tackle Philip Roth's *Everyman*. It could have been worse. The Roth originally selected for perusal was *The Plot Against America*, which I think may be a stretch too far even for someone with an English literature degree.

From my perspective, this isn't about continuing one's education, it is one-upmanship. Personally, I will stick with Gordon Brown. When I have finished (and even as I read it) I can discuss it, should I wish, with a friend who I know is reading it. And I can do so without taking notes, getting a babysitter or rushing home from work early to get to a book club in time.

Profit and loss

May 19, 2007

Personal lives should be just that, personal. My thoughts about the downfall of Lord Browne are many, but above all they are this: when will the journalists and their employers who sell so many papers from digging up salacious details about the personal lives of our business leaders learn that they are risking something much bigger than the ire of a few talented men and women?

The City of London is the leading financial centre of the world, and don't we know it. Everyone has a vested interest in making it stay that way, or so it seems. The UK government has convened a number of City luminaries to assist it in deciding what can be done to help the City stay at the top of its game and see off the likes of New York, or, God forbid, Frankfurt.

There are just over 3,000 companies quoted on the London Stock Exchange. These spawn an army of advisers including corporate brokers, lawyers and, of course, financial PR companies. Keeping all these people employed and on the doorstep contributing billions of pounds in tax revenues to the Treasury, and providing tenants for all the buildings, and customers for all the restaurants, is understandably a priority.

So what might topple London off its perch? Not, I would suggest, the lighter regulatory hand of Hong Kong or the cheaper commercial rents in New York. No, what will really make companies think twice before listing on the LSE will be the Fourth Estate. London, in comparison to New York, is a goldfish bowl. Annual reports are pored over for references to executive pay and options and the tall poppy syndrome is worse here than in Australia, where it started. In my day job I see up close how the reputation of senior executives can affect their professional lives. Men and women who have contributed millions - even billions - of pounds to the wealth of their shareholders are pilloried in the press and have everything from their pay packets to their personal lives dissected in over-familiar (and often inaccurate) language.

Setting aside Lord Browne, who helped to turn a once-moribund public-sector organisation into one of the world's greatest oil companies (no mean feat and a lot more than most journalists achieve in a lifetime), what do you know about Sir Martin Sorrell, creator of the WPP Group? If you live in the UK, then the answer is probably that he earns a lot of money, has recently got divorced, and along the way has had a relationship with someone in Italy. What you should know is that he has built a business over 20 years, almost from scratch, that is now capitalised at around £8bn. That takes talent, and effort, and should be rewarded. And if I had been a shareholder over those 20 years I wouldn't be worried what he did with his private life.

Personally, if I were the government and was seeking to make London the place of choice for companies to have their headquarters, I would shut down the business sections of some of the other weekend newspapers for a start; they have turned from organs of serious business reporting to somewhere between *Hello!* and *The National Enquirer*. There is a place for frivolity in newspapers, but it is in columns such as mine that people should expect to read about waxing regimes or the cost of a day's shooting, rather than in places that purport to offer serious business comment. Journalists who sensationalise business stories and turn captains of industry into celebrities for no better reason than to knock them down again should be reallocated to covering the UK's trade statistics.

So there you are. The Mrs Moneypenny Grand Plan to secure London for all time as the world's business and financial capital. Simply remove all the journalists who make our business leaders' lives such hell and replace them with sensible people who understand the concept of return on capital employed. Then Sir Martin Sorrell and his peers will stay here and others will join them.

Otherwise, I suspect we will see many people move their companies and their tax revenues abroad. For personal reasons.

Dogged in the pursuit of knowledge

May 26, 2007

I am fond of saying that arriving in Tokyo, a city I admire and adore, is the closest experience we can imagine to landing on Mars, so strange is it and so different from the rest of the world. Failing a trip to Japan, the next weirdest thing you can do is to attend an academic conference.

Academia really is a different world. There your worth is measured in published, refereed papers and citation rankings, not by where you come in the Rich List. As I don't feature in the latter and have very few published papers to my name, I am amazed to be welcome in either world.

But I am working on the refereed papers, at least, so I recently attended a worthy academic gathering for three days to present my work to date and have it scrutinised and debated by some of the finest minds in the field. All this took place in a three-star hotel in Corfu, which served food so dreadful that after two days I had to call my office and beg the Lovely Lucinda to find me somewhere else to stay.

Once you get used to all the facial hair (why is it that so many academics grow beards? And I am afraid this includes some of the women), it can be quite refreshing to debate the finer points of graph theory with some of the cleverest mathematicians on the planet. I learned a lot from them, not least about the ownership of animals.

The eminent professor I sat next to at dinner took a call from his wife in Boston. He then explained that she was going to take a shower, so he needed to excuse himself and go and log on to their home webcam. I thought this was really racy. They have been married for 16 years, but as they are without children I thought that perhaps her unclothed body was worthy of a webcam viewing. But no, it was not his wife in the shower that he was going to watch from a distance of 4,000 miles. It was their dogs, which she had put back in their kennels while she was in the shower. He therefore had a quick opportunity to view his beloved pets.

His wife had been at the conference for its earlier stages and the webcam was to allow them to check up on the dogsitter. How often were the animals being exercised? Were they being shut up for too long a period? Were they being fed on time? I can see that all these vexing questions were much easier to answer with a webcam.

The Moneypenny household dog is now back from gundog boarding school and I am looking forward to taking her out in the new shooting season. My first date is with grouse in Yorkshire on August 21. I didn't mention the grouse to the academics at first, as I didn't think that it said the right things about me. That was before another senior academic at dinner admitted to owning a string of polo ponies. Polo ponies, in my opinion, are not evidence of academic achievement, they are evidence of a private income. I took quite a shine to the polo-playing academic (who is single and at the University of the West of England, if anyone is interested - he is 42, way too young for me even were I available). He was also a longstanding reader of this column, it turned out. Was I what he expected? No.

Academics are always testing theories, and this one had two

about who the author of Mrs Moneypenny might be. His first idea was that there was a team of writers who took it in turns. I wish! No, it is just me, every week. His other theory was that the column is written by Nicola Horlick.

I have never met Ms Horlick, although from reading her publicity I suspect that she is too busy for something as mundane as a weekly magazine column. Or indeed for an out-of-this-world experience such as attending an academic conference in Corfu.

Pick of the crops

Jun 02, 2007

A hair appointment was essential on the day of the Chelsea Flower Show gala preview. For busy working women - and even busy and not- so-busy women who don't work - hair has to be the greatest single item of expenditure. Yes, more than shoes. More than handbags. And more than face cream. I know plenty of women who are prepared to buy cheaper bags, shoes and even face cream in periods of austerity, but will never compromise on where they have their hair done. And that is even when their hair is cut by Nicky Clarke and coloured at his salon, at a total cost of £530. He may be arguably London's most acceptable hairdresser, but I would have to have that done every six weeks, so annualised we are talking £4,240 and grossed up for tax the figure I would need to earn to fund such a habit is £7,067.

How you look is important, because you never know who you might meet. Or, in the case of the Chelsea Flower Show gala preview, you do know who you are going to meet - everybody. This year it wasn't raining, and so the guests spread out all over the place, mainly propelled by their wives who insisted on looking at the exhibits (Don't these women understand the real purpose of the event?). I had to walk three times as far to net my usual catch of chief executives, chairmen, finance directors and investment bankers. Regular readers may recall that I had invited not one but two FTSE 100 chief financial officers to join me, but they had both already accepted invitations by January 2, when I got in touch. Thus unencumbered, I was able to make at least two circuits before leaving and moving on to my next engagement.

You would be forgiven for thinking that any gathering after the Chelsea gala preview would be second rate by comparison. After all, the list of corporate heavyweights and dealmakers present took up three-quarters of the "People" section in the *FT* the next day. Yet I went on to something even more splendid - the Cartier dinner.

For this event I had had to summon Mr M. He met me at the gate of the Chelsea Physic Garden (venue for the Cartier dinner and a jewel in London's botanic crown that is but a few hundred yards from the flower show). He had been home to change into something more formal than his everyday workwear (style: relaxed wine merchant) and arrived in a bespoke suit (good), a pale blue shirt with double cuffs (good), and a very ordinary tie (bad, very bad). Why had he not selected one of the many Hermès ties I had bought him over the years? Or something by Ferragamo?

I whisked him inside, past the hordes of paparazzi, where my horror at his tie was slightly ameliorated by the copious quantities of champagne being served. But my horror returned with a vengeance after we were seated when - between the lobster salad and the lamb - I realised that Mr M was sitting not at all far away from Trinny Woodall.

Trinny Woodall, for those of you who have been living in Outer Mongolia for the past five years, co-hosts a television show and has co-written several books on the subject of what to wear (and not to wear). I can assure you that Mr M's tie would have been right up there had she needed an example of "what not to wear to a spectacular dinner hosted by Arnaud Bamberger, managing director of Cartier, on the eve of the opening of the Chelsea Flower Show, attended by guests ranging from members of the royal family to highly successful businessmen and peers of the realm both hereditary and elected". Even Mr M said afterwards that he half expected

Trinny to whip a tie out of her handbag and insist he put it on.

Next year, should I be invited again, I will personally select a suitable tie. Or even take a more suitable husband. Trinny's was seated beside me, wearing an exceedingly stylish blue Hermès number, no doubt personally selected by his wife. She was wearing her hair put up and adorned with items that complemented her dress. How our hair looks, if you are a woman, is critical.

Liberty belle

Jun 09, 2007

Some views of Wall Street. My first ever view was sitting with my Most Glamorous Girlfriend at the South Street Seaport in August 1987, and I have been back many times since. I remember all those hours in my former life spent in the meeting rooms of investment banks and fund managers, trying to flog some or other company's shares, looking out of the windows of some of the tallest buildings in lower Manhattan, in between justifying some tricky valuation model or market view.

I saw two totally different views of Wall Street during my visit to New York last month. One was at The Morgan Library, which is located at 225 Madison Avenue. Of course, you cannot see Wall Street from there, but you get a sense of its history. Not just because Wall Street helped to fund the restoration of the original library, and the building of the elegant light-filled structure designed by Renzo Piano that links it to the former Morgan family home, but because you start to understand what was important to Pierpoint Morgan way back then. Not for him new light-filled buildings; the ceiling of his study is a 16th-century structure that was shipped over from Europe.

And the books in the library itself, adjacent to the study? An eclectic collection of some of the rarest examples of the printed word. Is this what people did with Wall Street wealth in those days? Buy up, among other things, one of the most valuable collections of Bibles in the world? There are 59 copies of the Gutenberg Bible in existence - and no fewer than three of them are in the Morgan library. Now, I am a great believer in Bible scholarship, not just for moral guidance but because it informs so much else in our lives. But three Gutenberg Bibles? I am reminded of Luke 12: 16-21.

I was taken to The Morgan Library by a Canadian friend who moved to New York last year. He works almost on Wall Street itself, and must be almost as rare as a Gutenberg Bible - a straight, single, solvent 39-year-old man living in New York. His limited attempts at dating there have not been a success so far, which is why he was free to spend the weekend with me. And, as a qualified yacht master, he was planning to take me sailing in the Hudson river.

Now, I am useless at any mode of transportation other than driving a car. Take my most recent flying lesson, for example. Until now, my instructor has conducted all the dialogue with air traffic controllers and written the information down. My sole task has been to input numbers to instruments. Suddenly, with no warning at all, mid-air, I was passed the pen and paper and told to write down whatever numbers were issued. Needless to say, I failed to do this correctly which forced my instructor to have to call back Heathrow air-traffic controller and request that the information be repeated, which I am told was no good for his air cred.

So issued with a rope sailing halfway round the Statue of Liberty, and told to "cleat it", I was equally useless. I am not a sailor and unexpected use of a technical term is bound to cause immediate panic - especially when on a 24ft piece of carbon fibre dodging the Staten Island Ferry, a cruise liner, sightseeing catamarans and sundry craft in the Hudson on a Saturday afternoon. What is a cleat anyway? I was mightily pleased to be relieved of cleating duties and given the crisps and drinks to hand out. Being New York, these weren't real crisps, but "air-dried apple chips" which were a bit healthy for my liking. But I enjoyed eating them while hanging on to the rail for dear life while we tacked backward and forward during our trip out from North Cove. All the while looking back at one of the most spectacular views of Wall Street.

Weighty issues

Jun 16, 2007

Boredom is the enemy of exercise.

I work out at least three times a week, but I have to drag myself there and need constant variety to keep me going. Hence the need for Holly the Sadist, and hence the boxing.

Why do I bother? Probably because I find that exercise has so many benefits. It is the perfect antidote to depression, insomnia and low energy levels. I would like to think that I look better for it as well, but maybe I don't. On the Underground this morning, somewhere between Oxford Circus and Bank, a very kind middle-aged lady offered to give up her seat for me. It took me a moment to understand why and then I had to decide whether to embarrass her by explaining that no, I wasn't pregnant. I was just standing badly in an ambiguously designed dress.

Perhaps I should be working on my posture rather than my pulse. But that wasn't the most challenging attention drawn to my shape of late. Mr M and I took another couple to an open-air concert recently, and the husband had an interesting line in small talk during the picnic. He didn't mean to be rude, he assured me, but had I always been this size? His wife works for a large German bank and has to attend many corporate functions. Does she ever get him to accompany her, I wondered out loud? No, was the answer.

I am not surprised - as the evening (and the alcohol) wore on, I discovered that my weight was the least of the objects of his curiosity. Over the strawberries and cheese he asked me - in the same tone as someone might ask about someone's favourite book or holiday destination - what my favourite sexual fantasy was.

Now, Mr M may have his occasional lapse in the corporate husband stakes, but he has never asked any of my clients' wives to own up to anything more embarrassing than a failure to distinguish Bordeaux from Burgundy, so let's be grateful.

One of my other preferred forms of exercise is to go out on my bike, occasionally accompanied by one or other of my cost centres. CC#2, age 12, is particularly exhausting to cycle with.

Ten minutes into a cross-country ride the questions will start. Here is a selection from last weekend:

What is that algae? Answer: I don't know, let's take some home and look it up. How fast do glaciers move? I have no idea, look it up on the internet, what are geography teachers for, etc. Have you ever met Andrew Lloyd Webber? No, why on earth would I want to? Then the supplementary: How rich is Andrew Lloyd Webber? What on earth do you want to know that for, look it up in the "rich list".

I don't think I am cut out for childcare any more than I am for exercise. But HTS has recently decided to combine the two by setting up a Buggyfit class in Regent's Park. If I find the thought of childcare exhausting and struggle to bring myself to exercise, you can imagine what I feel about the idea of doing both at the same time.

Why anyone would wish to take their small cost centre, in a buggy, to Regent's Park to work out is even less clear to me than why anyone would want to know how rich Andrew Lloyd Webber is. Of course, at buggy age, cost centres are too small to ask tricky questions of their exercising mothers, so HTS shouldn't have to pause the proceedings to answer questions about Andrew Lloyd Webber. (By the way, should you ever have this problem, he is worth £750m, according to The Sunday Times Rich List.)

Mind you, by way of conversation topics, I am more relaxed about algae and Andrew Lloyd Webber than I am about my shape or my sexual fantasies. So I have every hope that CC#2 will grow up into the perfect corporate husband. Although I suspect that if such a thing exists, he might prove to be - like exercise - rather boring.

Card sharps

Jun 23, 2007

How accurate are your credit card bills? I was chatting to a hedge fund manager's wife at a drinks party last week and admired her handbag. She accepted my compliment graciously and then confided that she had bought it the previous week and paid partly in cash.

It seems that even if you are married to a man to whom the price of an extravagant handbag represents a bit of loose change, it isn't a good idea to have the whole cost appear on the credit card statement.

I was a bit taken aback by this, and recounted the story to the next woman I found myself speaking to, who is married to a private equity partner. She was not at all surprised - in fact she often did the same herself. I then called a few more woman I know who are married to similarly senior men and canvassed them, only to get the same (admittedly sometimes sheepish) reply.

How much is it acceptable to spend, as a non-working (or at least, non-earning) wife, on handbags, shoes, moisturiser and the hairdresser?

Perhaps readers can enlighten me. And what about the husbands in an equivalent position?

Mr M is far too busy playing golf to do anything so menial as scrutinise credit card statements these days, but maybe I should check them more carefully. He goes in for plenty of expenditure on essentials such as golf shoes, waterproofs and golf balls (obviously he picks the premium-priced ones where the manufacturer claims they can transform your game). Then there is all the en primeur wine that we seem to have accumulated in various bonded warehouses, and these were supposedly put on his credit card. After my credit card etiquette investigation, I am now wondering if he part-paid in cash for some of these purchases.

I also paid cash for some make-up this week, not because I wanted to disguise my spending, but because I had forgotten my Pin number for the credit card. Nevertheless, it was an amount that, were I married to a hedge fund manager, I might wish to disguise.

I spent £60 on a pot of foundation. Regular readers will know that my gripe with cosmetics is that they cost a lot but frequently carry inadequate application instructions. This time I made a point of going to the cosmetics counter for tuition, from the highly knowledgeable Justin at John Lewis in London's West End. It was just as well that I saw him because the written instructions with the foundation were practically non-existent, as well as misleading.

While the manufacturer suggested that I "apply using the fingertips", Justin's instructions were to apply using a special make-up brush (£30). If they want you to apply it with a brush, and even make and sell one, why tell us to apply the stuff with our fingertips?

I recently met a woman who has developed her business to a size that I can only dream about for mine. She is younger than me and blessed with skin that I envy even more than her success. But even she confessed to wearing make-up, and proved it by opening her handbag to reveal a decidedly unstylish Harvey Nichols plastic carrier bag containing a cumbersome load of expensive product.

What every successful woman needs is a second set of her most essential make-up, kept in something more stylish than a carrier bag. My Most Tenacious Girlfriend has taught me to carry mine in a neat Lulu Guinness bag that she bought me. But start thinking about two sets of make-up, a bag to put it in, the handbag to carry that around in - and it all begins to look expensive.

It is. When I complained in this column about the lack of instructions with a pricey moisturiser, I received a letter from a man at Goldman Sachs who passed on some advice from his wife. "She tells me that you apply it sparingly," he said, "although I am not sure how sparingly she applies it, given the bills I have to pay." Has he considered that the bills may be even higher than he thinks?

Labour after labour

Jun 30, 2007

My company is a little smaller than those featured this week in the FT Global 500. But it does have one thing in common with them. We employ a lot of women of childbearing age.

Currently, to the best of my knowledge, no fewer than four of our staff are expecting new cost centres this year. One of them is a man, and so he probably won't be away from work for too long, but the other three have the right to stay away for up to a year and get their jobs back at the end of it. If they take their full maternity leave, they don't need to give notice that they're coming back to work (though the Central Office of Information's Directgov website helpfully suggests that "it's a good idea to do so"). If, on the other hand, they decide not to come back at all, they can take the year to which they are entitled and then give us "notice in the normal way". Meanwhile, the business has two options: to spread the workload among others during their absence or hire temporary staff to cover.

It takes at least a year to learn to do what we do and be effective at doing it, so by the time we have trained someone, our staff member will - we hope - have returned. What is the solution? To staff up against the possibility of people going on maternity leave? That is effectively an insurance policy with a very expensive premium.

As it happens, I am in favour of maternity leave in principle, despite the burden it places on small businesses like ours. This is despite the fact that I was never very keen on it myself. I had tremendous difficulty coming to terms with the disruption that childbirth had on my life. I wanted children and wouldn't send them back (even though more than half our disposable income is spent on housing, feeding, transporting and educating them), but the practical side of giving birth and then caring for small babies has never had much appeal.

When expecting Cost Centre #1, I attended antenatal classes at the Pineapple Dance Studios in South Kensington because the classes were at lunchtime and minimised my time away from the office. But I wasn't a good pupil and was eventually expelled. One of the many reasons was my refusal to join in with "breathing practice". As I explained to the French woman who taught us and who each week grew increasingly exasperated with me, I wasn't going to take part in what looked to me like a very undignified activity. And anyway, I didn't need to - I was planning to have an epidural put in at eight months and carry on with it in place.

But it is important for women to bond with their cost centres - you never know when it might be helpful. Last week, for instance. CC#1, having finished his AS exams, bleached his hair in such a manner as to make him look like an association footballer. The school pointed out that term had three weeks to run and he was in breach of the rules. They informed me that he had to get it sorted out - or be excluded.

As he is up for election to prefect in his final year, I decided acquiescence was the best strategy. I called and told him to go to the hairdresser.

I was busy, and in my rush I managed to offend him. This resulted in him bypassing the hairdresser and trying to solve the problem with a cheap DIY dye kit. This in turn led to his hair turning an interesting shade of burgundy.

Maybe if I had breastfed him for longer than 10 weeks in 1989 and taken more than two weeks off work on maternity leave, he would have been more likely to respond positively to my original entreaty to attend the hairdresser near his school, which would have cost £42. By the time I had brought him up to London to get his hair restored to an acceptable colour by my own hairdresser, the cost was more like £80.

There are moments when I look at the smiling, happy faces of my expectant staff and wonder how they will cope when confronted by an outraged housemaster along with an unrepentant and recalcitrant bleached blond teenager in 18 years' time. I suspect these challenges are the same whether you are a working mother in a small company, or one in the Global 500.

Onion pickle

Jul 14, 2007

The onions were the deciding factor. I have little enough time as it is, what with work, children, husband and the readers of *FT Weekend* to take care of, and I do not wish to spend my weekends stringing onions. Cost Centre #3 (aged eight) was required to go into school suitably dressed for a "French breakfast". The accompanying note from the teacher helpfully suggested a striped top, beret and string of onions.

Onions? I go to France several times a year, for business and pleasure, but cannot remember ever having seen anyone in a striped shirt and beret with a string of onions around their neck - or cycling at the same time, for that matter. I know that such people probably do exist, but suspect that they are found in more plentiful numbers as stereotypes in children's story books.

If I were to send CC#3 anywhere pretending to look French I would probably kit him out in designer childrenswear, as the French seem to turn out impossibly stylish children.

But my issue is not with reinforcing national stereotypes, but with the burden on parents. Over the year that CC#3 has been at this school, I have been staggered by the level of parent participation required. There are "class mothers" who arrange social functions so that the mums can meet each other - a useful service for new parents to help them form friendships and support networks - but these events are usually held during the week and completely impossible for me to attend. Mr M and I did once go to a dinner at a local restaurant, but the food didn't arrive until after 9pm and since I have to get the 06:46 train each day I was agitating to go home to bed before the dessert.

Then there are the almost daily missives which arrive home in the school bag. Send money for this, fill in that, make a costume here, RSVP to a child's birthday party there. The past week has seen things reach a crescendo. In the space of six days we had five requests for parental participation. An after-school bowling expedition organised by the mothers (which CC#3 nearly missed because the note was sent by e-mail and found its way into my spam box), then the school sports day - on a

Tuesday - for which the instructions stated: "You will be present at 12 noon and you will bring your child a packed lunch." The day after that, an expedition to Cadbury World where another packed lunch (and £10 spending money) was requested. The evening of that day the class parents were going out for another gourmet dinner, and finally the French breakfast was the following morning.

Yes, I have a nanny to deal with some of this, but this is not a school with many working mothers, and nannies are rare. The stay-at-home mothers do not welcome the nanny into the fold, and why should they? My Hedge Fund Girlfriend tells me a worse story. The stay-at-home mothers at her daughter's London day school are all too ready to use her nanny when they have a crisis, but leave her eating M&S sandwiches alone with her charge, rather than invite her to join their outdoor eating extravaganza on sports day (HFG, like me, was not at sports day because it was midweek and clashed with a critical client meeting overseas).

I have had to face up to reality. I am not cut out to be a day school mother. With boarding school, you meet the other parents when you drop off your children on Sunday evenings, a time of the week which does not discriminate between working and stay-at-home parents. You will often watch sport with them on Saturdays, too. Meanwhile, sports days, speech days and other events such as plays are held in the evenings or at weekends, so one rarely has to miss anything. So CC#3 is off to boarding school next term. Yes, we will have to write off a term's fees at his existing school because we have not given notice. But that is a small price to pay for not having to string any more onions.

It's a judgment call

Jul 21, 2007

Are work appraisals worth doing? This was the subject addressed by my fellow *FT* columnist Lucy Kellaway a few months ago, and I was reminded of it because we are about to undertake our own.

I have always found appraisals to be a triumph of hope over experience. In my entire professional life, I have never had an appraisal that helped to improve my performance. I changed jobs so frequently during my eight years with a bank that I barely managed one, and since I joined my current business in 2000, no one has appraised me at all - and they are unlikely to start, considering I am now the majority owner.

I consulted my Most Tenacious Girlfriend on the subject. MTG is completely relaxed about being appraised by anyone on anything at any time because, she told me, she has had three unsolicited appraisals in the past seven days. The first was from her son's nanny on her dress sense. This highlighted various areas for improvement: less black, more colour, more patterns, more wow-factor. The only area where she scored highly was on handbags, which she felt quite pleased about.

The next was from a stranger on the flight to her summer holiday in Majorca and was on her parenting skills, or to be more accurate, her lack of them. The woman appraising MTG informed her that she herself had produced three immaculately behaved children and couldn't understand MTG's failure to stop her 18-month-old singing loudly and out of tune, or touching fellow passengers as he walked up and down the aisle.

What this woman didn't realise was that the only reason MTG was going to Majorca was to hand her son over to someone more capable than herself. She had found a nanny agency that sends British nannies there and to other Spanish resorts to work for holidaymakers. Had the woman been in possession of that information, I cringe at the prospect of how she would have appraised MTG.

MTG's third appraisal was from her husband on her literary tastes. She took on holiday the latest Man Booker Prize-winner, *The Inheritance of Loss* by Kiran Desai, described by the *FT* as "marvellous, poised and elegant" - hardly, as MTG pointed out to me, Joanna Trollope or Jilly Cooper. Her husband, however, would have preferred her to be reading *Sir Robert Peel: A Biography*, by Douglas Hurd, which he felt would improve her.

She had promised to read it, but just not that week.

The question is, will all these appraisals improve MTG's dress sense, parenting skills and literary choices?

I suspect that they won't. Nannies, strangers and husbands might find it easy to criticise, but managers at work often find it hard. A friend of mine observed that in places where he'd worked the managers were castigated for writing anything critical about the employees who reported to them. The reasons for this ranged from "it will demotivate them" to some sort of game theory. With an eye to the annual pay and bonus rounds, each department would need to suggest that it had the best employees and so deserved the most money. This would be hard to pull off if you criticised your own team.

He also pointed out that research had shown that organisations were skewed towards the favourable rating of their employees. Yet any reasonably sized organisation must have a normal distribution of abilities and achievements among its workforce.

We can't all be above average, as fund managers' performances regularly illustrate. So how honest - and therefore useful - can appraisals be?

In any event, he continued, in any post where a significant portion of pay is based on results - this includes most of the City and any sales job - the amount someone gets paid is a much better indicator of performance and a direct form of appraisal.

You might wonder in the light of all this why I am allowing appraisals in my own business. So does my friend, who claims I am addicted to democracy.

Not only am I the only employee in my business not being appraised this year, I also (within practical limitations) decide my own pay. Meanwhile, our business continues to grow, our clients return, our staff continue to stay. That is the only appraisal I need.

All change

Jul 28, 2007

Why haven't we joined the euro?

I know there must be lots of good economic reasons for holding on to our own currency but as I have said before, it is really irritating to have to change in and out of euros the whole time. The Lovely Lucinda dreads my trips across the channel as I complain yet again about the inconvenience of it all. She usually smiles sweetly, gives me a limited amount of cash and tells me just to use my credit card.

But that irritates me even more as my bank charges each time I make a transaction and the exchange rate varies from hour to hour. I am never really sure what I have paid for a hotel or a handbag until I return.

So I was one of the first applicants for the Caxton FX Eurocard, a pre-paid euro MasterCard that doesn't charge you for shop transactions in Europe. Yes, I know I have to pre-load it (and so they get the use of the money all the time I'm on the Eurostar and before I get to the shops) but I can reload free online and I know what the exchange rate was when I deposited the money. Why did no one think of it before?

Innovation in financial markets is the reason London stays ahead of the game, I was told by Sir Brian Pitman last week. Yes, personally. I was introduced to him at a debate at St Bride's on the future of the City of London and was reminded of the time I first met Sir William Purves. Like Purves, Pitman was a banker of such stature and repute that I was almost (but not quite) rendered speechless on meeting him. Was this the Sir Brian Pitman? The real one? The man who took Lloyds from a market capitalisation of £985m in 1983 when he became chief executive to one of more than £31bn when he left the job in 1997, without a rights issue? And for a salary that most people wouldn't get out of bed for? (He earned £467,000 as chairman in 1997.)

It would not be an exaggeration to say that Pitman himself was an innovator - he made banks an attractive investment opportunity again. For years they had been run partly for their customers and mostly for their employees, and shareholders never seemed to get a look in, other than when it came to yet another rights issue to pay for yet another international acquisition. He sold everything off, got back to basics and then engineered the merger with TSB, all the while staying out of the mayhem of Big Bang. Forty-nine years in one company isn't that fashionable these days either.

So I was fascinated to meet him and asked him lots of questions; it was like having a case study from my MBA days suddenly appear in the flesh and I made the most of it. I even got to kiss him goodbye when he left.

Sir Brian Pitman is 75. He remains on the boards of Singapore Airlines and ITV and is far from past it. But for how much longer is he going to go to debates in Fleet Street and meet star-struck columnists? You have to grab these opportunities while you can. I am constantly telling my children to make the most of the generation ahead of mine, because they won't be here forever and we have so much to learn from them. Older people are pieces of living history, and hearing about things first-hand rather than through the pages of a case study or a history book is so much more interesting.

At a wedding anniversary party recently (who has parties to celebrate their wedding anniversaries? Really.I regard this as a hostage to fortune, like giving an interview to *Hello!* magazine), I sat next to General Sir Robert Ford.

He graduated from Sandhurst in 1943 and then spent a year preparing for the Normandy landings.

As soon as I heard that I hung on to his every word, and they were all fascinating, especially to someone who only discovered second world war history in recent years and has read about 20 books on the subject since.

It did put my complaints about the euro into perspective, though. Arriving in Europe on D-Day, Ford had a little more to worry about than whether he had secured a decent exchange rate.

My friend, the cyber-huntress

Aug 04, 2007

My Most Glamorous Girlfriend is internet dating. Is that so terrible? She recommended the experience to another single woman the other day, whose response was "I am not that desperate."

As you know I find it somewhat bizarre that internet dating is regarded by some as desperate.

Cyberspace strikes me as the perfect place to find someone with whom you are compatible, mainly because you can screen out unsuitable candidates at an early stage without having to waste an enormous amount of emotional energy on them. I have fallen for people on sight only to discover later on that they were obsessive compulsives, or had read only one book in their entire lives, or liked Wagner - all of which I could have discovered had I cyber-chatted to them for a while before meeting them in the first place.

The really great thing, of course, is that you can specify what you are looking for in someone. Take this, for instance: "...must be young, handsome (I lay most stress upon a good shape), sensible, well-bred, chaste and tender, of some good nature, a great deal of generosity...". No, this is not an internet ad, but the beginning of a 1779 specification written by Thomas Hamilton, one of the founding fathers of the US, when he was looking for a wife. Solvency was also important to him: "As to fortune, the larger the better. Though I run no risk of going to purgatory for my avarice, yet as money is an essential ingredient to happiness in this world - as I have not much of my own and as I am very little calculated to get more either by my address or industry - it must needs be that my wife, if I get one, bring at least a sufficiency to administer to her own extravagancies."

Think how much easier it would have been for him to have been able to use the internet! But even MGG (whose extravagancies would have finished off Thomas Hamilton, I think) was initially reluctant - I had to drag her round to my office one evening, ply her with drink and then sign her up to two sites and pay for them myself before she agreed to go ahead. But once signed up, she embraced the process with enthusiasm, seeking out a suitable photo (not too glamorous, not too ghastly) and attaching it to her details.

The response was - literally - overwhelming. She had specified an age range of 50-60, so begging letters from mere boys of 35 were repudiated (despite the fact that several of them advanced the argument that they were likely to be more vigorous than people over 50). She set about whittling down the likely candidates from the 150 who applied to a list short enough to interview personally - eliminating the ones who reassured her that they still had their own teeth. From there she granted second interviews to a handful and then third and subsequent interviews to just one, who was divorced with a child of a similar age to MGG's child.

I have not met him yet but I have read his profile on the internet. He appears to be doing all the right things - whisking her away on her birthday for a romantic weekend and a Van Morrison concert, cooking her dinner, driving her to the airport at ungodly hours of the morning. I haven't asked about the sex, but if I learn that he puts his dirty laundry into the basket instead of on to the floor that will put the seal on my jealousy.

I met Mr M 20 years ago this month, and the internet didn't exist for the masses then. But we were still matched by computer - the Qantas computer that allocated us adjacent seats on the flight. We remain together, laundry habits notwithstanding. But if he ever puts me back on to the secondary market, I shall be rushing with enthusiasm - not desperation - to the internet.

Essex education

Aug 11, 2007

Mum, where is Essex? I have had some testing questions from my children, but this one from Cost Centre #3, age eight, on being told that I was going to Essex for the day to teach a one-off class to a group of university lecturers, did test my powers of explanation.

Essex, for those of you reading this in Seattle and Shanghai, is the county to the northeast of London. In the UK many people assume it houses professional footballers and their wives, and other people for whom elocution has largely been an optional extra at school.

It may surprise you to learn that Essex has the longest coastline of any English county. A straight line drawn parallel to the coast from the Thames in the south to the Stour in the north is about 50 miles in length but follow the convolutions of the coastline and you will cover nearer 400 miles. Once you get past the suburbs of such forgettable places as Chigwell and Romford and reach the sea, I have to admit that it is really rather attractive.

Every summer, the University of Essex plays host to a summer school, a six-week cacophony of learning. The quality of the teaching attracts postgraduate students and university lecturers from all over the world.

I assume it is the quality of the teaching because the aesthetic surroundings of the university are not appealing. It shares a birthday with me, having accepted students for the first time in 1962, but that's where the similarity stops. I am all curves and noisy personality; the University of Essex is all grey concrete and austere, angular architecture. As the Swiss girl showing me to the lecture room commented: "It's a sunny day and it's still depressing."

So I was determined not to be depressing in my one-hour lecture. This is not my only teaching stint - I teach on an MBA course each year in London as well - but it is hardly my main professional activity. I sometimes think I should give up teaching and take a one-woman stand-up comedy show on tour instead, but my children are horrified at the thought of a middle-aged mother of three making jokes at their expense and discussing the intimate details of the approach of the menopause (it is amazing how much more you notice advertisements for sanitary protection just as you are on the verge of never needing any ever again).

I get a lot of invitations to speak and accept relatively few of them. Essex may prove to be a one-off, as may the annual dinner of the Family Planning Association, which has me booked for a date in November. These days the FPA no longer runs the clinics it did when I was a student, which dispensed free contraceptives and asked no questions. Those clinics transferred to the NHS long ago. Now it is a charity producing and distributing educational literature on such compelling subjects as pubic lice and intrauterine devices. In particular it is keen to promote an open and informed discussion between parents and their children on the subject of sex. I cannot imagine why they want me as an after-dinner speaker.

My speaking engagements usually involve a few anecdotes, rather than jokes, as I know almost none. I even struggle to remember more than one "Essex Girl" joke. (For those ignorant of this tribe, last month *Time* magazine offered a neat explainer in a piece about Victoria Beckham moving to the US. An Essex Girl is "a lady from London's eastern suburbs who dresses in white strappy sandals and suntan oil, streaks her hair blonde, has a command of Spanish that runs only to the word Ibiza, and perfects an air of tarty prettiness.")

I last mentioned my Essex Girl joke in 2002, so here it is again five years later. Essex girl is involved in a car accident and is badly injured. The paramedics arrive, and before they cut her out of the wreckage, ask her where she is bleeding from. "I'm from bleeding Romford," she says. "Just get me out of here." Quite, I thought, as I escaped from the University of Essex.

On the mat

Aug 18, 2007

What is the point of Pilates? I attended my first Pilates class recently and am not sure I am any closer to answering the question. I have always considered Pilates to be up there with organic vegetables and natural childbirth - I am glad they exist, and that people have the choice, but they are not for me.

My Pilates-loving Girlfriend has been banging on to me for

several years about the benefits of Pilates and emphasising that the class she attends is close to our office. A few weeks ago I espied a photo of PLG in a glossy magazine attending some glittering social event and texted her to compliment her on her appearance. I jokingly suggested that if I could look like that I might even try Pilates. PLG's response to this was swift - she booked me in for a class.

So I found myself in a room full of machines that looked as though they had been imported from a medieval torture chamber and was confronted by a teacher so slim that she must have to run around the shower to get wet. And it wasn't even a "class" as I understand it - the teacher stations herself in the torture chamber for about four hours or so and people come and go in pre-booked slots with no more than five at a time contorting themselves in unnatural stretches while trying to breathe simultaneously.

Is this really how I wish to spend 90 minutes? I am not sure it counts as exercise. PLG, when sending me instructions as to venue and time and suitable clothing, said (assuming that it would encourage me) "you won't even have to take your make-up off". Quite. Even assuming I would have any on by 9am on a Friday, the fact that I wouldn't have to take it off shows that Pilates is never going to make me any slimmer.

I consulted my youngest sister before attending - had she ever been to Pilates? Once, was the answer, in Chiswick, and the class had been notable for containing elderly ladies passing wind during the most extreme contortions, and an actress from EastEnders. While my "class" did contain a range of ages, I didn't spot any celebrities and no one audibly passed wind. What did surprise me was how many men were present. The official Pilates website suggests that 25 per cent of Pilates students are men, but it was more like 50 per cent from where I was lying on the floor, trying to force my knees somewhere near my nose.

Comforting myself with the thought that the whole process might at least make me more flexible in bed, I considered whether Pilates was a suitable exercise for men. Is it really manly enough? I am told that all sorts of "real men" do Pilates, from the New Zealand All Blacks to the English cricket team, but I am not sure you would get Mr M off the golf course for long enough to work on his pelvic floor.

But what is suitable exercise for men? Many male political leaders seem to like running. French president Nicolas Sarkozy jogs in public at every opportunity. This has not always been seen as a positive attribute. French television has recently featured Alain Finkielkraut, a celebrated philosopher, pleading with Sarkozy to abandon his "undignified" pursuit. It would be much better, Finkielkraut suggested, if the head of state took up walking, like Socrates, Rimbaud and other notable men. George W. Bush also jogs, but I can't imagine anyone comparing him with Socrates.

Personally, I prefer my men in the gym sporting a pair of boxing gloves. Boxing is an excellent all-round exercise, building strength and cardiovascular fitness. Also, I am a great admirer of history and tradition. Not only was boxing apparently first accepted as an Olympic sport in 688BC, but the rules governing it have been in place since 1867, 13 years before Joseph Pilates (the inventor of the system of contorted exercises) was born in Germany. He emigrated to England in 1912 where he earned his living, among other things, as a boxer. It was only when he later moved to the US, the land of the jogging president, that he set up the first Pilates classes. He died at the age of 87, and so isn't around to debate Pilates vs boxing with me.

Our favourite things

Aug 25, 2007

What is your most precious possession? My children - despite being referred to as Cost Centres 1, 2 and 3 - are probably the most precious things in my life. But if I had to choose an inanimate object I'm not sure.

But my family know. This summer the UK had its worst July rainfall for 300 years and the subsequent floods afflicted, among other places, south Oxfordshire. One Saturday morning, after a particularly wet Friday, we awoke to find that you could sail a Sunseeker down our road and the water was moving purposefully towards our front door. On being summoned to view the scene, CC#3, aged eight, immediately and without discussion shot downstairs, unplugged the PlayStation and removed it and all its leads to a place of safety on his top bunk, itself in a room on the first floor. He then put a towel outside the door for good measure.

Mr M, unsurprisingly, set about the speedy task of removing every piece of sporting equipment from the path of the flood. After making sure that every cricket bat (these can cost £200 to replace) and golf club (the most recent purchase - one club, please note - was £250) had been taken to somewhere likely to remain dry, he set about the task of digging channels away from the front door to divert the passage of the water.

The water did invade, but thanks to the trench digging and the sandbags it never got to more than a few inches high. Apart from taking out the ground-floor electrical circuit and ruining all the carpet and underlay, it didn't cause too much chaos. The flood never threatened the item that Mr M considers the most vital to his everyday life - the Sky box.

This is the box that sits under the television and lets us receive satellite TV. We buy such extensive packages of programming that, when I last looked, we seemed to be funding almost all of Rupert Murdoch's working capital and I am not surprised that he has managed to find the cash to buy Dow Jones. You could buy a healthy size provincial newspaper, I calculated, simply by securitising the Moneypenny subscription stream, let alone the millions of others.

As I watch very little television - I confess to enjoying *The Apprentice* but as this is on BBC1 I hardly need a Sky box to see it - I do not understand the passion excited by this piece of plastic with a few cables sticking into it can excite. But Mr M's latest discovery is that there is yet another subscription-only channel he can add to the monthly bill that will allow him to watch live Australian Rules football. Of course! How did we exist before? It often starts before 6am, but no matter; he sets his alarm and is off downstairs before dawn on a Saturday to press the satellite TV into action and watch 100 minutes of action from 12,000 miles away.

The commitment to satellite TV showed itself when I last went away for a 10-day business trip and returned to find that no post had been opened at home - with the exception of the Sky statements. On questioning, this was because Mr M was worried that the correspondence might be last-minute demands for payment or something else that might threaten the uninterrupted supply of sports programming to our house.

Our electricity loss because of the floods could have been a disaster: it was the weekend of the England-India test match at Lord's and the British Open at Carnoustie. Fortunately, Mr M's trench digging meant sports programming was available by the next morning (and the physical activity of trench digging gave him an early night).

We are currently away in Edinburgh where CC#1 is appearing in a rather modern production of Jason and the Argonauts. It is not raining, there is no flooding, and we are on the fourth floor of the hotel, so I feel safe. But I fell asleep last night with golf on the screen. Nothing, it seems, can stand between us and satellite TV.

It's us and stem

Sep 01, 2007

I like flowers. I like them in the garden, even though I have not the faintest idea how to grow them and I especially like them in vases in my office or at home. Should any of you wish to send me flowers, my favourite colours are cream, yellow and white, but I do not enforce these prejudices in the office, where our flower monitor is the Lovely Lucinda.

Flowers did not figure in LL's original job specification. As befits a small company, we buy and arrange our own flowers, rather than outsourcing to a contractor. This task used to fall to the most junior member of staff, who would head off on

Mondays with some petty cash to the nearest flower stall and return to put their purchases into vases. This arrangement worked well until we hired a particularly chippy graduate who made it plain that flower arranging had never been part of her career plan.

Fortunately for her, the Lovely Lucinda arrived and said that she would like to assume this responsibility. LL was not taught flower arranging at finishing school, but instead has a number of books on her desk that inform her displays. The results look quite good to me (I was particularly taken with a blue effort in the reception area recently) but we encourage all our employees in self- improvement and so when she asked to go on a flower arranging course recently, we agreed.

At the end of the two-day course LL won first prize for her final arrangement, a photo of which she sent to me and at which I briefly glanced.

It looked very complicated, unlike anything I had ever seen before, and my immediate reaction was to consider entering it for the Turner Prize.

On investigation, it turned out that LL had been on an underwater flower-arranging course. No, this did not involve her arranging flowers with mask and snorkel, but arranging them in such a way that they were displayed while submerged.

When, I asked, were we going to see one of her underwater creations in the office? LL prevaricated, saying they took ages to construct. Fine, I said, just come to work earlier. Then LL explained that they only last a day. Fine, I said, she would just have to come to work very early all week.

How impractical can you get? I can barely believe that we approved this training. I have suggested to LL that perhaps she would like to go on a more useful course, something like "Flowers for Reception and Meeting Rooms That Last a Week and Don't Cost the Earth", but apparently such a course doesn't exist. Instead, she tells me, she wants to do a course at Jane Packer, round the corner from our office - on wedding flowers.

After LL went home that night, I inspected the course schedule left pinned above her desk. There appeared to be different wedding flower courses, entitled Stage One, Stage Two and so on. I can quite see that flowers for second marriages need to be different from those for the first, and for third marriages even more so - no wonder they need different courses. LL herself has had a starter marriage, so presumably she needs to go on the Stage Two course, but currently she does not even have a boyfriend, so I have no idea why she wants to learn how to do wedding flowers. Whatever next?

Ante-natal classes for people who are thinking of coming off the pill?

The next day LL explained to me that the different stages are not for different marriages. Stage One includes such compelling subjects as "bridesmaid pomander" (what the hell is that? do we care?) and an "overarm bridal bouquet" (the idea of an underarm bridal bouquet boggles the mind, don't you think?). Stage Two, by contrast, raises us to the heights of competence to execute a "beaded tiara" as well as a "wired bouquet". The only wired thing at my marriage was my bra.

The course is going to occupy LL every Tuesday night from late September into the winter.

It seems a long while - yet again - to spend on flower arrangements that last only a day. This time, however, LL will be paying for it herself.

Swing Out Sister

Sep 08, 2007

Sun, sea, sand - and golf. The Moneypenny family will, by the time that you read this, have returned from our holiday. Not for us the crowded airport terminal, or the overpriced beach hotels on the Mediterranean coast. No - we will have been to the Hebrides to play golf.

When I say "we", I mean Mr M and me and Cost Centres #2 and #3. Cost Centre #1 did his own thing this year, renting a flat in Portugal with friends and then returning to take a play to the Edinburgh Fringe Festival, in which he played Under-Argonaut #43 in *Jason and the Argonauts*.

After its week-long run, when his fellow Argonauts returned to England, he stayed on, moved into someone's spare room and worked for a fortnight as an unpaid reviewer on the festival's main publication, *Three Weeks*. This proved a very worthwhile, if lonely, occupation for a 17 year old.

The night before his AS level results, he called me at 10pm. "I am tired, lonely, hungry, stressed about my results tomorrow and on top of that I've got to go and sit through the spectacle of a bunch of Australian transvestites performing *The Sound of Music*." By 11.30pm, when he called back, he was sounding much cheerier, particularly about the transvestites ("best show I've seen so far").

The next morning, at 9am (9am?! I didn't know it featured in his body clock outside term time), he sounded even more positive as he informed me he had obtained four As. Once I had ascertained this was not a joke, I had to sit down to recover. Clearly it is possible to fit academic work in between drinking and socialising, after all.

We will have had to have set off with the golf clubs before his return. Let's hope Mr M's back is up to playing. He has been walking around bent over, looking more like 80 than 50, and visiting the osteopath regularly. Why? Because his golf teacher has taught him a new swing, and it has put his back out.

I have examined the small print of our health insurance and am not convinced that "a new golf swing" will swing it, so to speak, with the claims department.

After Loch Lomond, Oban (well, Glencruitten Golf Club) and a couple of nights on Mull, we will have spent a week on Colonsay. There is a links course on Colonsay, although it does not allow visitors. You have to become a member. This requires payment of the annual fee, which can either be made at the local pub or at the estate office. I am not anticipating having to liquidate any assets to fund this - it is £20.

We may have to liquidate some assets, though, to pay for the other golf club membership that Mr M plans to take up this year. After no fewer than eight years of waiting he has been elected to membership of the Royal Sydney Golf Club. This is even further away from south Oxfordshire than the Hebrides, although the transport is more frequent - ferries to Colonsay leave only three times a week and the airport does not open to commercial traffic until October.

While we are on the subject of transport to Sydney, did any of you see the latest set of results from Qantas? In January, you may recall, I lamented the prospect that Qantas looked likely to be sold to private equity, and said that I did not think it would prove to be the finest hour of the chairman, Margaret Jackson. True, the airline's performance needed attention, but as the new owners did not even plan to change the chief executive, what were they going to do that could not be done under public ownership?

For those of you who have not followed this, the shareholders rejected the deal, the chairman subsequently announced her retirement from the board and the airline has just reported a stellar set of results. Hoorah! Mr M and his golf clubs will be heading off again for a few weeks soon, this time alone - to Australia, home of sun, sand, sea, golf, Qantas - and transvestites who perform *The Sound of Music*.

A COLLECTIVE MEMORY FAILURE

Sep 14, 2007

September 15 will be a day of celebration for the people gathered for the marriage of two friends. It is his second and her third, so by now they should know how to throw a party, and I'm sure it will be a day we remember.

Some 67 years ago, in 1940, September 15 became a day of celebration for millions. This day is now commemorated - albeit decreasingly so as that generation dies out - as Battle of Britain Day. The largest concentration of enemy aircraft ever seen came across the English coast that day, but was defeated by the Royal Air Force's Fighter Command, whose airmen had been so famously praised by prime minister Winston Churchill a few weeks previously: "Never in the field of human conflict was so much owed by so many to so few. "

Last time I referred to a historic figure in this column, Alexander Hamilton (1755-1804), I mistakenly called him Thomas. The only good outcome was that many of you wrote in about it, and it was good to "meet " you all. Many Americans owe much to Hamilton, not least those who work on Wall Street - he helped found the Bank of New York and promoted the development of the New York Stock Exchange. It is no surprise that there are many statues to him, one of the finest in Central Park.

Here in Britain, we are not quite so good at commemorating our heroes. In my opinion there were three principal architects of the historic victory that was the Battle of Britain: R.J. Mitchell, Air Chief Marshal Lord Dowding and Sir Keith Park. Mitchell designed the Spitfire, the legendary aircraft, and there are many tributes to him, including statues in Stoke-on-Trent and at Solent Skies museum in Southampton; busts at Southampton university and the RAF Club, London, and a memorial stone on the site of the Supermarine works, Woolston. There is also my favourite statue of him, by Stephen Kettle, at the Science Museum in London.

Dowding is commemorated by the famous statue in the Strand, outside St Clement Danes church, where my friends' wedding reception will be today. I commend it, and its inscription, to those of you who have a spare moment. (Goldman Sachs in London - you're nearby. Now that the markets have slowed down and there are fewer pressing deals to be done, why not walk up and take a look?) There are also memorials in a park in Moffat, Dumfriesshire, the town of his birth; in Royal Tunbridge Wells where he died; and there is a bust of him at Winchester College, where he went to school. His ashes are interred in Westminster Abbey, and the Dowding Centre at the School of Fighter Control at RAF Boulmer is named after him.

But what of Sir Keith Park? A New Zealander by birth, who had survived two of the bloodiest battles of the first world war, he is, in my opinion, perhaps the most influential of the three. I am not alone. In 1947, Lord Tedder, then in charge of the

RAF, said: "If any one man won the Battle of Britain, he did. I do not believe it is realised how much that one man, with his leadership, his calm judgment and his skill, did to save not only this country but the world. "

What memorials are there to this man, whose marshalling of men and machines ultimately put paid to Hitler's goal of invading Britain? Well, there's an aviation collection and a school in New Zealand, a road named Keith Park Crescent in Biggin Hill, Kent, and ... er ... that's it. I think this is a disgrace, and before Sir Keith Park's memory is extinguished, let us correct it. I see that the personal interests of our current Air Chief Marshal, Sir Glenn Torpy, include military history (as well as hill walking and cabinet-making), so perhaps I should try to meet him and press my case. I'll keep you posted.

As far as I am aware, apart from the crescent in Kent the only UK memorial to Sir Keith Park is locomotive number 34053, one of the Battle of Britain class, commissioned by the Southern Railway in 1947. After a series of owners, and being sold at one point for spare parts, it is now safely in the hands of Southern Locomotives Limited, a not-for-profit organisation that restores, maintains and runs steam locomotives.

Southern Locomotives sells shares in individual locomotives, so I am buying shares in the Sir Keith Park, at £250 each (www.southern-locomotives.co.uk). This may prove an even more illiquid investment than a US sub-prime mortgage derivative, but will give much more enjoyment as I follow the progress of the restoration - which I will try to visit on or near September 15 each year.

I don't mean to grouse, but...

Sep 22, 2007

Last month, I threw a £12,000 dinner party for eight guests. Did I take over a top London restaurant? No. Did I fly everyone to Paris? No. The venue was a comfortable if unexceptional hotel near Saltburn-by-the-Sea (never heard of Saltburn-by-the-Sea? You and many others. Look it up). The guests travelled there at their own expense and not one of them would have had a journey of less than three hours.

We were there because I hosted a day's grouse shooting. This is an exercise in risk management. First, you have to book the day itself. Early season grouse days for people who don't own their own moor are in limited supply and late days, when available, are not released until the close of the season - by which time most of your potential guests will have filled their diaries.

The guests themselves comprise the second risk. Many of the people I would like to invite would have filled their diaries for August by the previous January. I then need to find eight people who would be interesting enough for their fellow guests to meet, congenial enough to spend 24 hours with in close confinement, interested in shooting grouse and willing to travel to Saltburn-by-the-Sea.

It is hard enough to secure people who are sufficiently interesting to spend just two hours with and who are willing to travel to Chelsea on a Monday afternoon in May. Yes, it is not just the grouse season that has started. We are already into the Annual Chelsea Flower Show Gala Preview Guest Grab. One finance director whom I asked last year (but had already accepted an offer from an accountancy firm) already has an invitation for May 2008. I have not even heard if I have been successful in the ticket ballot yet, let alone invited anyone. I had better get cracking.

For my expedition to Saltburn, I assembled a very acceptable group: two chief executives of large quoted industrial companies, a notorious investment banker, a hedge-fund manager, a ridiculously handsome PR adviser, the manager of a rock band and a (female) British dress designer. Plus someone who is slaving away as an executive director of a public company because an accident of birth has left him the owner of a stately home that needs a lot of maintenance.

Guests secured, the next risk to manage is the grouse. Booking the day and paying the deposit will not ensure the presence of these birds. Good gamekeeping and the careful management of both sheep and grouse on the moors can help to preserve enough grouse for sport, but there are no guarantees and the weather plays a part in the eventual result. The agent helpfully sent gloomy forecast after gloomy forecast in the months before, thus managing expectations. Rain and floods wiped out entire grouse populations in several places but miraculously, in North Yorkshire, the birds survived and were present in suitable numbers by August.

We gathered the night before for dinner, and enjoyed a convivial meal and several bottles of wine ahead of a good night's sleep, a hearty cooked breakfast and then a drive to the moor. And there we stood, peering at each other through the fog.

Yes, the fog. We could barely see 10 yards. We had picked the one place in the British Isles on August 20 2007 where coastal fog enveloped the landscape so comprehensively that any attempt to shoot a grouse would probably have resulted in us shooting each other instead.

I had booked the day, secured the guests, picked somewhere that disease and flood had spared the grouse, and yet we never took a gun out of a slip. Instead, we stood around for a while hoping for the fog to clear, retired for lunch (our third meal together), reviewed the visibility and then we all went home.

Not so much a £12,000 dinner party as a £12,000 dinner, breakfast and lunch party. In the spirit of the Chelsea Flower Show, I am about to send out my invitations for next year. Saltburn-by-the- Sea, September 1 2008, anyone? Investing in subprime mortgage portfolios looks risk-free by comparison.

When will she be famous?

Sep 29, 2007

What is the definition of a successful woman? Each year the *FT* Magazine examines the achievements of women across Europe and the world who have risen to positions of influence.

I aspire to be included in this hall of fame, but suspect that my definition of success may be different to theirs. I feel successful for having organised transporting Mr M and Cost Centres #2 and #3 to the Hebrides for a week or so. (Why is it that even when you have a full-time job your husband still expects you to do all the household administration? Ferry tickets, hotels and self-catering cottages don't appear by magic.) No matter, we made it, and, among other expeditions, went to look at the one place I know of in the UK that is a little piece of Australia.

Lachlan Macquarie (1761-1824) was the first military governor of New South Wales and grew up on the Isle of Mull, which is also where he is buried. The mausoleum and the land it stands on were gifted by a Lady Yarborough in 1948 to the people of New South Wales, 12,000 miles away. Financial responsibility for this little piece of Scotland is now with the National Trust of Australia.

Given that NSW has a population of about seven million, more than half of whom live in Sydney, it's a fair bet that most of them have never heard of Mull or know anything about this generous donation. Mr M is an Australian citizen, and a New South Welshman, so I thought a visit was appropriate.

The weather in the Hebrides sadly does not resemble that of New South Wales, but what the two places do have in common is some really lovely and largely deserted beaches. Incidentally, I regard it as another measure of success if I manage to get Mr M and all participating Cost Centres on to the beach, in either the Hebrides or NSW, having remembered to take all relevant kit out of the car. Bucket? Spade? Fishing net? Towels? Sunscreen? (These last two, I am afraid, were not needed in the Hebrides.)

On one occasion in Scotland, I had locked the car and was heading for the beach when Mr M asked me for the keys. He then told me that although we had got all of the children's stuff out of the car, he had forgotten his sandwich.

Now, my hearing is not what it was before I took up shooting, but I promise you that is what he said. I looked incredulously at him for a moment. Even assuming that he would think to bring food along, it is more likely to be a packet of wine gums.

Mr M does not do packed lunches, unless it is for an occasion that he considers important - eg a child's sporting event. Even then you have to buy all the ingredients and tell him where they are and where the lunchbox is to put them in. (Why is it that, even when you a have a full-time job, your husband expects you to organise the acquisition of packed lunch ingredients?)

Of course he hadn't made a sandwich. He had brought along his sand wedge. So while our mini-engineers were constructing complicated systems of water channels in the sand on a remote beach in Scotland, he was using the time usefully to practise getting balls out of bunkers.

I don't do packed lunches, either.

I do, at the weekends, do a considerable amount of cooking. (Why is it that, even when you have a full-time job, your husband expects you to cook almost all of the meals?) I do this on an Aga, a cooker which is (a) on all the time (b) has fixed temperature ovens and (c) no grill. And no, I do not (unlike most other Aga-owners) have another cooker. If I can't cook it on or in the Aga, it doesn't get cooked. It comes as no surprise to me to learn that while there are 10 Aga shops in Scotland, there is only one in Australia.

I turn out pretty good tucker (as they would say in NSW) on my Aga. And that makes me feel successful.

Even if the *FT* hasn't included me in its hall of fame.

The state we're in

Oct 06, 2007

Where did you go to school? The Sutton Trust, a respected educational charity, published UK research last month showing that a disproportionate number of students at the top universities came from an "elite" group of 100 schools.

This was not the usual rant about how Oxford and Cambridge are running preferential admissions procedures.

Sir Peter Lampl, the charity's founder and chairman, was at pains to point out that there was no suggestion of "skulduggery". Exam grades are not the problem: many children in state schools get A-levels good enough to win places at the best universities, he said.

So what makes the difference? The Sutton Trust research showed that the "elite" schools prepared pupils better, gave them better "soft skills", encouraged them to read more widely and developed stronger interpersonal skills and other non-academic advantages. In addition, these schools encouraged their pupils to aspire to higher levels of achievement, and the pupils were supported in this by their families. This was something that didn't happen in many state schools.

None of this came as a surprise to me. What I did marvel at was the extent of the research. The charity analysed university admissions between 2002 and 2006, involving more than one million students from 3,700 UK schools and colleges. That's a lot of data. Sir Peter is a worthy man and he has donated a lot of money to his charity, which has done much good, but did he need so many statistics to come to this conclusion?

Basic economics could have given him the same answer. About 80 per cent of the "elite" schools named in the report are fee paying. Only 7 per cent of pupils in the UK go to a fee-paying school. Yes, as the Sutton Trust found out, this can confer huge advantages.

I think many of us know this already. Why else do you think we pay such extortionate fees?

I am often accused of using adjectives lightly, but extortionate is the only appropriate word for private school fees in Britain. Markets work. If you have a premium product, you can charge accordingly. Sir Peter didn't need to analyse a million student records - he could just have come and asked me why we pay such a high proportion of our net income to educate our children when we already are paying, via tax, for the state education system.

It's a question that I could well ask myself. Cost centre #3 has now been outsourced to boarding school and CC#1 still has a year to go before he leaves, so this is going to be the most expensive year of our lives in terms of school fees. Think of the holidays and the houses we could have afforded if we hadn't signed up for this. Commenting on his report, Sir Peter lamented the way in which the class system hampered the progress of children in state schools, because it lowered their aspirations. But we used to have an education system that offered class mobility - grammar schools. They were abolished as elitist, their opponents arguing that they removed the chance of a glittering future from those who didn't pass their 11-plus.

They have been replaced, in effect, with something even more elitist. Many people of my generation and older, who were educated in high-quality state schools, are having to pay to give their children the education that they got for free. Interfering with markets is always dangerous, and may have unexpected consequences, as the Bank of England has recently found. Anthony Crosland may have vowed to destroy "every fucking grammar school" but not only did he not succeed (a few remain), his Education Act of 1968 has left us with a very undesirable consequence, as Sir Peter's report showed.

While we wait for a Conservative government to be elected and restore the grammar school system (or not, depending on who in the Conservative party you ask), there are other initiatives that seek to raise the educational aspirations of schoolchildren. The UK Career Academy Foundation, for example, leads and supports a national movement of employers, schools and colleges working to raise the aspirations of 16 to 19 year-olds, and our little business supports its work. I am determined that CCs#1, 2 and 3 will not be the last children whose aspirations I try and help to raise.

Some enchanted evening

Oct 13, 2007

People usually remember me if we have met. This is not something to boast about, as it is often because I have offended them by being too loud or saying something inappropriate. And I meet lots of people. I have a job that requires me to speak to and meet anything from 10 to 50 new people every week.

So it should have come as no surprise that I had previously met the investment banker I was seated next to at a wedding recently. Except that it was a surprise to me. I introduced myself, and he immediately said, "Oh, but we have met before. You write a column in the *FT* and run a small business in London." I looked at him more closely. I had definitely never met him before. As opening gambits by over-confident investment bankers go, claiming to have met me before is pretty brave.

I admit I am not good at remembering whether I have met celebrities of the *Hello!* magazine variety. They all look the same to me. I am slightly better with minor members of the royal family and a bit better still with members of the cabinet. But investment bankers? They are of great interest to me, only pipped at the winning post by the finance directors of public companies. I always remember meeting them.

There are, of course, investment bankers that I have never met but remain ever hopeful that one day I will. Top of the list is Anshu Jain. Apart from breathing the same air once in a crowded room at the Grosvenor House hotel, I have never been near him, let alone been introduced. Why is this? How many more hints can a girl make?

I hear he is keen on cricket - after 18 years of marriage to Mr M I could not be better qualified to make conversation with Anshu Jain.

Sadly, it was not Anshu Jain that was seated next to me at the wedding. It was a man who runs the UK operations of a leading non-British investment bank. I knew who he was, of course, because I had seen many photos of him in the newspapers.

These photos are invariably of him on his yacht in the Caribbean hosting famous guests to whom he has occasionally lent swimwear.

He was entertaining and charming company, which was nice - after all, getting stuck next to a tedious investment banker at a wedding would have been a dreadful bore. But all the charm in the world could not change the fact that we had never met before. And as for his knowing that I was a businesswoman who writes a column in the *FT*, there must have been 20 people in the room who could have told him that.

Eventually, our discussion became so heated that the man sitting opposite asked if we were married. Married couples arguing at weddings is a much more common event than my forgetting that I have met an investment banker. On my right was seated the finance director of a public company, by chance the one I've mentioned here before who has already been invited to the Chelsea Flower Show. I introduced him to the banker, using a great deal of detail, most of which I had gleaned over the years from my occasional reading of the tabloid press. And certainly not from ever having met him.

Information on people is never hard to find. This particular banker, for example, owns the url of his own name - as in www.firstnamesurname.com. On it, I note, he has published his business card, including his mobile telephone number, so if you want to call him up and ask him which famous guests he has invited on his yacht this year, you can.

But I will save you a call. The Moneypenny clan will be in the Caribbean this winter, and we have been invited to be the guests of this banker. Whether we will be borrowing his swimwear, I don't know - though it was mentioned in the offer. Whether this banker is either (a) deluded about having met me, or (b) so instantly forgettable that I genuinely couldn't remember our meeting, I also don't know. But neither theory looks attractive. No matter, we shall accept. Unless there's a cricket match at which Anshu Jain craves my presence.

A citizen speaks out

Oct 20, 2007

I am never short of opinions, as you might have noticed. Occasionally I am invited by some foolhardy person to share them in public. Thus it was that I came to take part in a recent debate on who would be the best mayor of London for business.

Greater London has had an elected mayor since 2000, when Ken Livingstone won the first ballot, and he then went on to win re-election in 2004. There will be another election next year. Mayor Livingstone has far fewer powers than, for example,

Mayor Bloomberg has in New York, but far more control than he has over critical issues such as transport and planning. Plus he is supposed to promote London internationally. Of course an elected mayor is by no means a new concept. The square mile or so that forms the City of London has been electing its mayors since at least 1189, when Henry Fitz-Ailwyn held the position.

On the day of the debate the Conservative party confirmed that its candidate for mayor to run against Mr Livingstone next year would be the journalist and MP Boris Johnson. Mr Johnson is known, among other things, for his untidy hair, outspoken comments and political incorrectness. As I pointed out at the debate, if I had realised that these were sufficient qualifications for public office, I would have put myself forward as a candidate.

I did prepare some comments, but as I spoke last and the three other speakers were professional journalists, I did not need my notes. I simply pointed out some inherent flaws in their arguments, all of which were very supportive of Mr Livingstone and not very supportive of Mr Johnson. Journalist number one cited as an example of Mr Livingtone's success with the business community the fact that the financial district had readily accepted the congestion charge. On what basis did he argue this? In my experience, no one in the financial district even knows what the congestion charge costs. If they can afford to drive into the City and park, their PA usually sorts it out.

Journalist number two said he wondered about Mr Johnson's ability to deal with pressing issues that were dear to the business community, such as airport expansion. As I understand it, the City is far more interested in the expanding heliport facilities near Canary Wharf and the imminent arrival of a fab restaurant at Battersea Heliport than it is with an additional runway at Heathrow.

Journalist number three suggested that Mr Livingstone should be preferred to Mr Johnson because he had done the job before. On that basis, no one else need apply and we won't bother with the expense of an election. Let's just keep Mr Livingstone in office until we eventually have to have him embalmed. Or perhaps stuffed.

During the debate I was delighted to see Toby Young filming it for publication in his video diary of Mr Johnson's campaign, which appears on the *Spectator's* website and also on YouTube. Delighted for two reasons - one is that Mr Young is a writer whose work I enjoy and whom I had not previously met, and second because I have yet to make my debut on YouTube.

Mr Young wrote a popular book called *How To Lose Friends & Alienate People* which is being made into a feature film starring Simon Pegg and Megan Fox. The book portrays him as a bumbling social misfit who manages to offend almost everyone he comes into contact with. My experience of meeting Mr Young was that he presents much better in 3D, but perhaps appearances can be deceiving.

The next day I eagerly tuned into his video report of the debate to see if my witty repartee and pre-debate visit to the hairdresser made a suitable impression on screen. To my horror I had been entirely cut from the edited report! Journalists one, two and three, all of whom were male and none of whom had bothered with the hairdresser, featured heavily. You can make me out in the distance in the establishing shot and then from time to time you catch a glimpse of my shoulder. The most you will see of me is when I accidentally move into shot for a nanosecond while reaching into my handbag for my BlackBerry.

Mr Young has recently been to New York to spend a day on the set of his film as an extra in a party scene.

I wonder if he will make it into the final cut or, like me, find himself consigned to the cutting room floor.

The turning tide

Oct 27, 2007

Wealth creation is good for everyone. People who create wealth - for themselves and others - through starting and building up businesses deserve to be encouraged. Entrepreneurship, it is commonly agreed, is good for the economy. Business schools all over the world strive to teach it.

For most of the past decade, entrepreneurship in the UK has thrived. This has been in no small way due to the very favourable tax regime introduced in 1998 with the arrival of taper relief, something that sounds rather like a weird intestinal treatment but is in fact a rule that allows people selling business assets to pay a tax rate as low as 10 per cent on their capital gains.

This has encouraged lots of people, including me, to invest in businesses. Let me explain. I have, say, £100,000.

I can invest it on the stock market, and must then hope that the shares will go up. I don't have to do anything - just watch the share price. I could be sitting on the beach, going out shooting or simply reading a book. However, if the shares do go up and I decide to sell, I pay capital gains tax at 40 per cent.

If, on the other hand, I invest that £100,000 in starting a business, lease premises, hire staff, work 18-hour days and most weekends, and the value of the business goes up, I can sell it (provided I have owned it for two years), and pay capital gains tax at 10 per cent.

The second option is clearly far harder work than the first, but it creates more jobs and puts more money into the economy. Hence it is rewarded with a lower tax rate.

Now, we hear, we are to have one tax rate, regardless of whether you took the beach route or the 18-hour-day route. And you don't have to wait two years or even two minutes to qualify. It doesn't take a rocket scientist to work out what will happen next. See you on the beach.

Taper relief has been lauded as one of Labour's most successful initiatives. Why, then, abandon it? The answer is that there has been outrage in the UK at how a small number of people working in private equity funds (as opposed to people working in companies backed by private equity) have used this incentive to pay low tax rates on sums of money that many people believe to be income. This has got so out of hand that the government is now using a Draconian measure to deal with what it perceives to be an abuse of the tax system.

Now, I believe in private equity. It has an important role to play in providing capital for business. I like many of the people I have met who work in it. I met an especially nice one out shooting the other day. (If you were a conspiracy theorist you might have a view on the credit crunch coming just at the start of the shooting season, allowing all these private-equity types to abandon their deal-making for a few months while they take up their guns.) But I am incandescent at being penalised for their excesses by a government that can't work out (or cannot be bothered to work out) how to deal with this in a more targeted fashion.

In between trying to reduce the partridge population of southern England (my aim became far more accurate when I imagined every bird I saw was a tax inspector), I asked my charming private-equity companion what he thought of the plan to abandon taper relief. He observed that the measure was likely to cause rather a lot of collateral damage. My dictionary describes that as "injury inflicted on something other than an intended target". Exactly.

And worse - this rule will not come into effect until April. I saw several accountants quoted this week recommending that people sell before then. So now employees all over Britain who own shares bought via standard "save as you earn" schemes - most of whom have never had anything to do with private equity - will sell shares in the companies that employ them just to beat a tax deadline. Managers, we know, achieve the best returns for shareholders when their interests are aligned. To achieve that alignment we need them to hold more, not fewer, shares in their companies and to hang on to them. But the incentive to do that has just become much smaller.

In effect, the tax rate on speculation will halve, and the tax rate on entrepreneurship will almost double. Looks like that beach is going to get very crowded.

Who let the dogs in?

Nov 03, 2007

Unexpected guests can have unexpected consequences. Early in the year, if you are fortunate, invitations for the forthcoming shooting season arrive from a variety of people - investment bankers, headhunters, public and private companies, and even from private individuals lucky enough to own an estate. You consult your diary to see if you can accept. Although I could be (and have been) accused of being in the "martini" camp of sporting guns - anytime, anyplace, anywhere - most people I know apply some quality control to their invitations. If you are CEO of a large public company you will receive so many invitations that to accept them all would be impossible.

So you accept the ones from people you like and the ones where the other guests are likely to be fun. After all, time is scarce - why spend 24 hours being bored by people you hope never to see again?

Assuming you accept, a few weeks before the event a letter will appear with directions, details of the accommodation, a polite enquiry about what gauge of shotgun you use (for cartridge supplies) and - crucially - a guest list. This allows you to swot up (what did we do before Google?) and also to make sure that you are up to speed on the status of anyone with whom you happen to have any business relationship with. I also share guest lists with people in my office, so that they can see that I am spending my time with useful people and not just on yet another corporate jolly. (As if. It's hard work, all this eating, drinking and standing around in the glorious English countryside.)

On one recent shoot my host omitted me from the guest list - by mistake, he says. One of the other guests, who escaped exclusion, was someone my business partner vaguely knew.

At the shoot dinner I sat next to him and introduced myself. He told me that, despite my omission from the guest list, he had known I was joining the party. His wife had told him. This had, apparently, been the cause of a challenging domestic exchange along the lines of: "I hear you are shooting this week with the girl who runs a company with X."

"What girl who runs a company with X? There are no girls on the guest list."

"Well, I heard from X that her business partner was going to be on the shoot, at dinner and staying in the hotel with you - are you sure? Is there any reason you would wish to keep this from me?"

"There is no reason and there is no girl - look, here is the guest list. Check for yourself, you will not find her on it."

And so on.

But unexpected women are less of a problem than unexpected dogs. Many of you have written to enquire about the progress of our dog, a beautiful black Labrador bitch that we sent to gun-dog boarding school over the last shooting season. The answer is that I have taken her out on three days so far this season (less than a third of the days I have been out myself - it beats working for a living) and she has enjoyed it very much.

But on the shoot that had me as the invisible guest, I hadn't realised - until I set off armed with the map placed in my hand by the Lovely Lucinda - that our digs for the night were not the usual stately home or comfortable country pub, but the new Four Seasons Hotel in the aptly named Dogsmerfield. As I drew up at the front door and handed the car keys, guns and luggage over to a bevy of butlers, they looked askance at the dog. The manager was summoned. "Madam," he said, "may I ask how much your dog weighs?" I confessed that weighing my dog was not something I did very often - I don't like weighing myself, let alone the dog. He thrust a letter into my hands.

"The hotel is prepared to accommodate your pet, provided that it is less than 7kg and less than 45cm to the shoulder." It went on to say that the dog had to be appropriately restrained "as defined in Defra Animal Welfare (Control of Dogs)". As neither of us had a set of scales, a tape measure or access to a copy of Section 10(2) of the 1991 Dangerous Dogs Act (which defines a "public place") we decided to give her the benefit of the doubt.

Lying about your weight is a skill every woman needs to

master early on, but they probably don't teach it at gun-dog boarding school.

A MONUMENTAL EFFORT

Nov 10, 2007

How best to remember the dead, particularly those who died defending their country? This year Armistice Day falls on the very date - the 11th day of the 11th month - on which the armistice was signed in 1918 between the Allies and Germany at Compiegne, France.

The agreement, for the cessation of hostilities on the western front, signalled the end of the first world war. Many nations will use the occasion to remember those who made the ultimate sacrifice.

The Royal Air Force was in its infancy when the war ended - it came into being officially on April 1 1918. There were still casualties, even in that short time, and they are all commemorated in a memorial in St Clement Danes, the London church that serves as the central church of the RAF.

One day last month I stole a few moments of a working day to spend some quiet time in St Clement Danes.

A beautiful book is displayed under glass in the crypt, open at that day's date. When anyone who has ever served in the RAF dies, their name is set down on the relevant date. For October 25, when I was there, two names were inscribed in perfect copperplate.

I was very moved by the church, originally built in the 10th century, rebuilt by William the Conqueror a century later and then pulled down and rebuilt several more times, most notably by Wren in 1681, before the Luftwaffe did for it in 1941, leaving only the steeple and walls. The interior of the church was rebuilt and dedicated to the RAF in 1958. I commend it to you.

One plaque contains the names of all the first world war casualties but the second world war claimed the lives of more than 116,000 men and women of the Air Forces of the

Commonwealth. We will never know the final resting place of many of them and they are remembered on memorials at El Alamein in Egypt, Singapore, Malta and Ottawa, Canada. Those lost from bases in the UK and northern and western Europe are commemorated at the Air Forces Memorial in Runnymede. Appropriately, this moving place overlooks the Thames and the field where Magna Carta, the document that sets out man's basic rights under law, was signed by King John in 1215. I am not given to quoting Queen Elizabeth II, but the dedicatory speech she gave in October 1953 is displayed there and is worth borrowing from as we remember the fallen this weekend: '' … for as long as freedom flourishes on the earth, the men and women who possess it will thank them … ''

Back at St Clement Danes, several other books commemorate particular sections of the RAF. I was drawn to the one that lists everyone killed in action in the Battle of Britain, defined as those from the RAF and the Fleet Air Arm, which were under the control of Fighter Command between July 10 and October 31 1940. You may recall from a previous column that I remain astonished that Sir Keith Park is not personally commemorated - Park ran the air defence of London and south-east England, and it was largely thanks to him that so much of London, including so many Wren churches, remains with us today. The Battle of Britain monument on the Embankment bears his name, but no statue of the man himself exists anywhere.

Since I wrote that piece, on Battle of Britain Day, things have moved on. A benefactor has offered (through the letters column of the *FT*) to underwrite the cost of erecting a statue, and a campaign is under way to position it on the vacant fourth plinth in Trafalgar Square, at the heart of the city that Park saved and within sight of New Zealand House (Sir Keith was born in New Zealand).

Trafalgar Square is under the control of the Mayor of London, Ken Livingstone, and he has delegated the decision on what occupies the fourth plinth to a group of commissioners, who seem convinced that what London needs is a series of increasingly abstract works of art. None of those commissioners could enjoy a free London now were it not for Sir Keith and those who served in the RAF in the summer of 1940. Perhaps we, and they, should listen to our monarch and thank those who fought so hard for our freedom - and what better way to do so than with a statue of Sir Keith Park?

To join me in campaigning for the statue, write to the Fourth Plinth Commissioning Group, c/o Greater London Authority, City Hall, The Queen's Walk, London SE1 2AA.

Blade runner

Nov 17, 2007

My car is 18 months old and has 32,000 miles on the clock. I don't even drive it to work every day - I sleep in the office at least two nights a week and my commute then requires me merely to walk downstairs. The reason my car has done so many miles is largely because I drive to so many shoots.

Reaching the spectacular scenery of Scotland or west Wales, or the high pheasants of Exmoor, or (greatest treat of all) the grouse moors of Yorkshire, tends to involve a long and tedious drive. Flying with a lot of kit that includes a gun can take even longer unless you use a private jet, and even then the airport is often still some distance from the shoot.

The sensible thing would be to travel by helicopter. At this time of year, many of the helicopters flying out of the London Heliport in Battersea are bound for shoots, for the most part chartered by people who are cash-rich and time-poor. I may not be guilty of the former - all things are relative - but the latter certainly applies to me.

My announcement that I might charter a helicopter to travel to my next shoot, on the borders of Shropshire, drew dire warnings from some of my less enlightened acquaintances, particularly those working in the media. Surely helicopters are unsafe? Aren't we always reading about them falling out of the sky? This is the kind of sweeping generalisation that betrays nothing but ignorance. Helicopters are actually very safe. Mile for mile, you are far more likely to die driving down the M5.

Most helicopter accidents are due to pilot error, according to the Civil Aviation Authority. But reading the accident reports, it seems to me that most pilot errors arise from flying in inappropriate weather. Moral of the story? Don't bully your pilot into flying in poor conditions. Bear in mind the old pilot's adage: take-offs are optional; landings aren't.

The reason that helicopter fatalities get so much press attention is because they usually involve someone rich or famous or both, viz Chelsea Football Club vice-chairman Matthew Harding and champion rally driver Colin McRae. Because helicopters are expensive to run, they are always likely to be carrying someone at least vaguely newsworthy. This is not the case with cars and even aeroplanes - which crash far more frequently and involve many more casualties.

Those of us without the privilege of owning a helicopter have to charter them from commercial aviation companies.

I called David McRobert, group MD of PremiAir, which operates the London Heliport, to ask if I was likely to crash on the way to Shropshire. This provoked a torrent of facts and figures delivered in a way that suggested he had reached the limits of his tolerance with ignorant journalists. I will simply summarise that "helicopters are very safe".

I believe him. When I recently visited St Clement Danes, the central church of the RAF, in London I noticed a plaque dedicated to the memory of those who have died in helicopter search and rescue operations in the past 20 years. It bore two names.

So, I am even keener on helicopters now than I was before.

But there is a problem with helicopters that goes beyond ignorance of how safe they are or why they crash.

The heliport at Battersea is the only one in London and is restricted to 6,000 take-offs each year. This is in sharp contrast to New York, which has many more. Such a lack of an essential executive travel tool in London is all the more amazing given the City's valiant efforts to wrest dominance of the world's financial markets from Wall Street. An aversion to helicopters would seem to extend beyond the media and into the mayoral politics of London - the Mayor of London, Ken Livingstone, believes that investment in buses is preferable to any airport expansion. This is of no help to those, including Richard Gooding, MD of London City Airport, who would like to see a second London heliport.

Back at Battersea, there was one helicopter-related question that McRobert couldn't immediately answer.

What about the dog? The dog? he asked. Yes, the dog. Having shelled out £2,000 on gun-dog boarding school I am making sure that she gets to as many shoots as possible. One of my fellow guns the other day told me that he transported his dog in his Robinson helicopter and that she (the dog) loved it. Would PremiAir take my dog?

McRobert's office came back to me to say that they would take a dog in "special circumstances". These seem to be that she should be on a lead and be accustomed to noise. Marvellous. That's fewer miles in the car next year, then.

Sound advice

Nov 24, 2007

Technology is a great help to the ageing.

I include myself in that category; at 45 years old (and counting) I need plenty of technology to help me through the day. Indeed, even with all the usual devices littering my handbag (mobile phone, BlackBerry, strange gadget for remotely accessing my *FT* e-mail, remote control to lock the car, and so on) I am thinking of adding some more - a pair of hearing aids.

I have suffered from otosclerosis in both ears for at least a decade. For those of you who can't be bothered to look that up, it means that the smallest bones in my body, the stapes (or stirrup bones) are gradually ceasing to function.

I could have surgery, but that's a big step and I have yet to get my mind round the question of how to manage the time off. Until I can handle that, I may alleviate some of the symptoms by wearing hearing aids.

I have tried them out before, twice - in 1998 and again in 2001. Each time I gave them back because I found them hard to get used to and convinced myself that I could manage without.

I can hear most frequencies fine, but if you have a low or gentle voice, or ask me a question from the back of the hall, I can't hear you.

I suspect I have been held back for the same reason many others have - vanity. Hearing aids can be seen as a sign of weakness, old age, or of being deficient in some way. But I have now been inspired, from the most unlikely quarter, to have another go.

I had breakfast a few weeks ago with the Last Unpaid Chairman of the London Stock Exchange. He did that job for 13 years for no remuneration - why? "It was a form of public service." That was in the days before the Exchange became a public company. The current chairman received more than £300,000 in the last financial year.

LUCLSE may not have made any money in that job, but he has gathered up enough to buy two hearing aids, which he puts in or removes according to need. I was very impressed both with his deft use of the devices and with his willingness to discuss them. He tells me, "The great thing about them is that they are optional. If you have them in, you can switch between speech, music, a setting to muffle the traffic or any other loud noise (I leave this to your imagination) and the loop (which I haven't used); you can vary the volume, and you can have one ear on, or both, or neither, all at the flick of the not-so-remote control."

While I am trying to imagine what loud noises might need to be imagined, I am doing something that I need no hearing assistance for - enjoying LUCLSE's book of photographs, *These Fragments*, published in 2005, in which he records the things that he encounters as he walks in Ardtornish, in the west of Scotland.

Before they emigrated to Australia, the Moneypenny forebears lived in and around Ardtornish, and the family grave is in Lochaline cemetery, so I can claim to have an interest, rather than just being a groupie. Plus, it is much more digestible for laymen than some of LUCLSE's other offerings - *English Barometers 1680-1860: A History of Domestic Barometers and Their Makers and Retailers* being one example. I will never understand how that one made it to a second edition. There must be a lot of keen students of the barometer out there. Not that I begrudge LUCLSE his success in publishing: after 13 years of not being paid for doing a very grown-up job he needs to earn a crust somehow.

Mr M has been moaning for ages that he needs an eye test. He has brought up the subject from time to time, hoping, no doubt, that I will get the hint and book him an appointment with the optician.

I have so far resisted. However, he recently managed - unaided - to find his eye-test voucher, book and attend an appointment and buy two pairs of glasses, all within 24 hours of arriving back from three weeks in Australia.

What, I asked, had happened to get him there at last? It turns out that he can no longer see where the golf ball has landed, and that isn't because he is hitting it so much further. Good to know that I am not the only member of the Moneypenny family who needs technological help with failing faculties.

Nifty ways to leave your lover

Dec 08, 2007

Breaking up is never much fun, even though these days there are lots of different ways to do it. Take Cost Centre #1, for instance. A few weeks ago he finished with his girlfriend. He did at least do this by telephone, rather than by e-mail or (worse still) text message. But having put down the telephone, he went straight on to the internet, and altered her official status on his Facebook page.

Apparently this relayed the news automatically to everyone linked to his page as a "friend" - some 300 people.

I have to say it makes me glad my teenage dating took place in the pre-internet years. It is bad enough to be handed your

P45, but far worse to have 300 people notified of the fact within 30 minutes.

Anyway, CC#1 is now single, or, as his Facebook page says, "not currently in a relationship".

The Lovely Lucinda is also not currently in a relationship. This is not because she is working so hard for me, what with having to pay my congestion charge and recover my laptop from taxis. It is not even because she is spending so many evenings on her course in bridal flower arranging. In fact I am not sure why LL is single, since she is very beautiful, gracious and kind, and delightful company. While she has been working for me, she has had at least two reasonably serious relationships, but neither of them has come to much.

Like many, if not most, of my single girlfriends, she has also tried internet dating with mixed success. Recently, irritated with her lack of progress in finding someone to marry, she took a week off work and registered with a very upmarket dating agency. Did it need a week? LL tells me that it was a very long and detailed process, with lots of form-filling and an extensive interview.

To me that sounds more like a VAT inspection than a process likely to end in matrimony, but what do I know?

LL also had to write a thumping great cheque to the dating agency (more similarity with a VAT inspection). This, I was told, represented a serious investment. Sacrifices would have to be made.

But then LL hit on a novel way of paying for the dating agency. A few weeks earlier, she had bumped into her first husband at some party or other. Yes, LL had a starter marriage. I have never inquired into the causes of its demise but it seems to have been reasonably amicable, although she had not seen the chap for five years. He, though, clearly remains very fond of LL, asking after her wellbeing and wondering whether there was anything he could do for her.

Put on the spot, she couldn't think of anything. (That's the difference between us. Should any ex-boyfriend ask me that question, I would think instantly of a list of things starting with a grouse moor and ending with a Hermès scarf.) But after thinking about it for a few days, LL rang her old flame and told him that, yes, there was something he could do. Would he please pay the bill for the dating agency?

This doesn't seem unreasonable to me. As her first husband isn't going to be the person to father LL's children and take care of her for the next 40 years or so, he could at least help to find someone else to do the job. Indeed, such a practice could even become a new kind of outplacement. Every divorcée should be offered this service - along with anyone in a long-term relationship when it comes to an end.

I can see great potential in this. LL inadvertently may have hit on a very practical solution to (a) the guilt of the departing party and (b) the problem of being put on the secondary market and having to find someone new.

Incidentally, her former husband agreed to her request immediately, took her out to dinner last week and handed over the cash. I shall keep you posted.

So perhaps CC#1 should have offered to pay for his girlfriend to join an internet dating service by way of helping her with her outplacement? Maybe. Though telling 300 Facebook friends that he has broken up with her amounts to pretty much the same thing.

Know me, know my wishlist

Dec 15, 2007

Christmas is approaching fast and presents are starting to weigh heavily on my mind. It will come as no surprise to regular readers that it falls to me to oversee present administration in the Moneypenny household. Including, invariably, my own.

Don't you just hate it when your nearest and dearest says: "What do you want for Christmas?" I wonder how many of you smile sweetly and say: "Whatever you would like to get me, darling, just something small. Don't go to any trouble," when what you are dying to say (if you are me) is: "I can't believe that you've asked me that - again. How can you have been married to me for 19 years and still have no idea what I would like as a present?" I mean, really.

I like presents. I like giving them and I like receiving them. I put a lot of thought into the presents I give and I am invariably disappointed when people - well, let's not beat about the bush - when Mr M either does everything at the last minute or forgets completely. The fact is that the best presents are unexpected - after a column in which I lamented the absence of ensuite bathrooms in stately homes I received no fewer than three dressing gowns in the post from readers. (I particularly liked the lime green micro-fibre one from Italy, by the way.)

Being too busy (ie having too much golf to play) is no excuse for failure to come up with a present. I know very few people who are busier than me and I still manage to find the time to go shopping. Birthdays, Christmas, Valentine's Day, anniversaries - I mark them all with one glaring exception:

I am notoriously bad at remembering the birthdays of my godchildren.

I have five godchildren, by my reckoning. I had already reached an age at which taking on any more would have been a stretch (after all, you want to be around to see them grow up) when Single Girlfriend produced a baby. This, you understand, was not a unilateral act, though she has still to marry its father and they have just had another one. I found her invitation to take on godchild number five impossible to refuse. Two of my godchildren are adults and are fending for themselves. The other three are the offspring of Most Glamorous Girlfriend (Guy, aged nine), Longest Standing Girlfriend (Samuel, aged seven) and, as I mentioned, Single Girlfriend (Louis, aged one). I don't know why I am so bad at remembering their birthdays, and it will be my resolution for 2008 to do better. I shall hand the task of ensuring my improvement to the Lovely Lucinda.

We give Christmas presents at work, also. There are about 20 of us (depending on the alarmingly high pregnancy rates in the office) and we operate a "Secret Santa" scheme in which everyone draws the name of a colleague for whom they will buy a (small) present. When the recipient opens it, we all have to guess who the giver was.

This ritual is one reason why our Christmas lunch necessitates spending a whole afternoon in a restaurant in Islington. Yes, Islington. We used to move venue each year and then a few years ago we found the perfect location, where we could take over the whole place and make as much noise as we like. And we like to make quite a lot of noise.

I hope Helen Bailey, CEO of Islington Council, is reading this. A few weeks ago I gave an after-dinner speech in which I made clear my (wholly subjective) view of Islington as a place where everyone eats organic vegetables and reads *The Guardian*. She was in the audience, and came up afterwards to introduce herself and defend the good citizens of Islington. I was rather taken aback, not by her forthright defence but because she was so much more glamorous than I imagined your run-of-the mill local government CEO would be. I hope she will be pleased to read that I shall be eating organic vegetables and opening presents on her patch on December 19. Even if I won't be reading *The Guardian*.

I shouldn't give Mr M too hard a time. He has been known to come up trumps. About two years ago I received a bicycle for my birthday - exactly the sort of bicycle I would have bought for myself. But I don't need another one, so this year I hope that he walks down Bond Street, rather than Bike Street. Something made of white chocolate, a seriously upmarket black pashmina to use on the plane, jewellery of any kind, anything from Hermès…

Job done

Dec 22, 2007

Outsourcing, as regular readers know, is a subject close to my heart. I outsource Cost Centres #1, 2 and 3 to boarding school; I outsource as much of Christmas as I can; I outsource dog training to gundog boarding school; and I have even looked at outsourcing the Lovely Lucinda to India, where her administrative tasks could be carried out far more cheaply, though the downside, of course, would be that none of us would receive a weekly briefing on the intricacies of bridal flower arranging.

But the best outsourcing idea I have had in the past two years was the suggestion I made in June 2006 that we should delegate the British criminal justice system - at least in relation to white-collar crime - to the US.

Since then, the US has held two trials of British citizens for white-collar crime, one of which involved the "NatWest Three", who have pleaded guilty to one of the charges against them and cut a sentencing deal that is likely to see them jailed for 37 months in February. The plea bargain has yet to be ratified by the trial judge - and there have been cases where that has not happened, so their sentence may yet grow longer.

When I last touched on the NatWest Three, a full-page advertisement had appeared in at least one national newspaper. It carried a letter, signed by several businesspeople, which argued that Messrs Mulgrew, Bermingham and Darby should not be extradited to the US. I wonder what those people think now of the letter they signed? I have not seen many of them rush into print to defend their stance at that time. But perhaps I should not be surprised.

I can see no reason for trying to prevent the extradition of the NatWest Three. There was a compelling case against them (which everyone seemed to ignore at the time). But an even more persuasive reason to send them over there was that the Americans are so much better than the British at securing convictions for white-collar crimes. Why not outsource their trial to the US taxpayer? They paid, and even better, they got a result!

The trial of Lord Black was another fine example of a US prosecutor securing a conviction for a white-collar crime.

Here was a British citizen, who headed a notionally Canadian company and had defrauded shareholders all over the world. Fortunately, someone came up with a good reason to try him in Chicago. After 14 weeks of testimony from scores of witnesses, the presentation of 700 documents and 12 days of jury deliberation, Black was convicted of obstructing justice and three counts of mail fraud, and his co-defendants were found guilty of mail fraud. And please don't forget the guilty plea from his former henchman David Radler, part of another sentencing deal. I call that a result.

I think this is all very good business for the Americans, and no doubt a deliberate strategy to help prop up their slowing economy. The throng of journalists, lawyers and other interested parties that has descended on Houston and Chicago will have injected a good deal of money into the hospitality industry and also resulted in plenty of revenue for mobile phone companies. Houston in particular is on a roll - the latest news from there is that in another case, covering price-fixing, the US has in effect handed the Office of Fair Trading its first successful cartel prosecution on a plate by getting the three British defendents to plead guilty before returning to the UK for sentencing.

If I were President Bush I would have a team working full-time to seek out white-collar crime overseas that can credibly be dealt with on US soil. This would be a much better policy idea than trying to fix the interest on subprime mortgages via legislation.

We in the UK may not escape all involvement in the NatWest Three case, since they may end up serving part of their jail sentence here at our expense. But compared with the cost and hassle of a British trial, we have done pretty well out of the whole affair. The conviction will act as a deterrent to people in the UK, as will that of Conrad Black. And we didn't even have to do the work ourselves.

As an outsourcing idea, it is one that has proved pretty effective. When I last wrote on the subject, I even suggested the US might not be the only place to look to - why not Saudi Arabia, which has the advantage of a full range of sentencing options? But I guess that would be going too far. As would outsourcing the Lovely Lucinda to India.

Birds, bees and speakers' fees

Dec 29, 2007

So, farewell 2007. When I look back, how will I remember you? Probably as a year of business progress, family progress and a considerably greater number of public speaking engagements.

As Mrs Moneypenny, I have had - and accepted - more speaking invitations in 2007 than ever before. Why do I bother? Partly because I meet new people, partly because I donate all the fees to charity and so it is a good way of turning my time into useful cash for someone, and partly because I am always looking for new readers. And it can be an entertaining way of passing an evening. My speaking engagements this year have taken me to all sorts of places I haven't visited before, such as the great hall in Lincoln's Inn, one of the four Inns of Court in London that form the ancient seat of the English legal system.

I was there to address the annual dinner of the Family Planning Association. The interesting question at this point is probably not why I accepted such an invitation but why did they ask. I suspect the answer is that (a) the retiring chief executive, Anne Weyman, is a chartered accountant (and a jolly smart one - she's going to have some spare time soon so all those of you who need someone to chair your audit committee, form an orderly queue) and, as such, she reads *FT Weekend*; and (b) the association's strapline for its new campaign is Talking About Sex.

The Cost Centres groaned when I told them I was going to address a gathering hosted by an organisation that is running a campaign to encourage parents to speak more openly and more often to their children about sex. "Mum, we want you to talk to us less about sex, not more," was the plea from Cost Centre #2.

I had been planning to write a speech but then the association sent me a sample selection of their brochures and I realised that there would be no need, as 16 of them deal with contraception. (New party game - name 16 methods of contraception.) One of these was entitled "Natural Family Planning". This sounds to me a grandiose title for what I used to call "crossing my fingers". I am told that, correctly practised, it is 98 per cent effective. By the time I had read in the brochure what one is supposed to do to practise it correctly, I was surprised it wasn't 100 per cent effective - after you have messed around with thermometers and become an expert on assessing the texture and transparency of bodily fluids, you certainly wouldn't have any time left for actual sex.

Reading out the instructions took up a fair proportion of the 10 minutes I had been allocated to talk about sex, and I then turned to their brochures on sexually transmitted diseases. By the time I had read out all their titles, I didn't think anyone in the room was ever going to need contraception again. The variety and impact of what you can catch these days is more than alarming.

At the end of my speech I auctioned off a chance to have breakfast with me in aid of the charity, at which the winner can talk about sex or, indeed, anything else, for an hour. Remarkably, the highest bidder was not some unsuitable man but a married woman. When I reported this to the staff in my office the next day, they took great delight in showing me a picture on the internet of her husband - a drop-dead gorgeous Olympic rowing champion.

I suspect she bid for the breakfast as a way of making a legitimate charitable donation, rather than because she really wanted to share scrambled eggs with me. But I live in hope that she will take up her purchase - and bring along her gorgeous husband, too. Now there's something to look forward to in 2008.

Profit of doom

Jan 05, 2008

Happy New Year. What does 2008 hold for you? I am never confident of predicting anything other than death or taxes, but one thing that I do confidently predict for me this year is that I am going to have to go through a refinancing.

Thankfully we are not talking about a massive writedown of dodgy assets followed by a desperate plea to some or other

Sovereign Wealth Fund to buy mandatory convertible stock in Moneypenny Enterprises. It is just that our original facilities, put in place to allow me to lead the buyout of our company, will have run their allotted course and must be replaced. This will involve a pleasant conversation with the bank manager, followed by the submission of our accounts and the exchange of a few legal documents. No, I forgot - we have to find a new bank.

We have been sacked by ours. Why? Not for bad behaviour, I can assure you.

Our crime is that we are too small, or rather, considering we have doubled in size since we did the original deal, that we need too little money. Our bank has worked out over the past few years that it takes just as much time and effort to process a credit for £5m as £50,000 or £500,000 (funny that), and so it has decided to set £5m as the minimum it will handle. But we don't need a working capital line of £5m and I haven't seen anything for sale that is worth anything like that much. Indeed, having cast an eye over some other companies in our sector, we decided that a start-up made more sense than an acquisition, and doing that cost us a lot less than £5m.

So now we are not a customer of our bank so much as a rounding error. And at some point in 2008 I shall be trudging about explaining our business model and future prospects to a number of banks that are happy to work with a small business.

Actually, I could talk about our business all day, so proud am I of what it does and the people who work for it. But it will take a lot of time, and given that our financial year end is towards the middle of the year, it is likely to coincide with all the things I would rather be doing - the Chelsea Flower Show, Ascot, Wimbledon (I have already been invited to the Final - how efficient is that for invitations?), Henley and the Cartier polo, to name but a few.

How is a girl supposed to get through all that and meet endless bank managers as well? Looks like 2008 is going to be a busy year.

Down to earth

Jan 12, 2008

Visiting New York is always appealing.

In mid-December, I went for 24 hours and managed to make every minute count. Here's how: fly in late at night and go straight to bed, then up early to deal with the day's e-mail before sallying forth into the Manhattan day. An excellent breakfast on my own in a random cafe in mid-town reading the *FT*; three business meetings; three visits to important shops (including, with express instructions, The World of Golf); a wander round the Robert Capa exhibition; then an early dinner and home again, sleeping overnight on the way back.

What makes a dash to New York a really palatable proposition, as I have said before, is that you don't need to use Heathrow. When Silverjet launched, I said in this column that a good reason to fly with it was that the chief executive, Lawrence Hunt, was rather attractive. But I acknowledge there are at least two flaws to this line of reasoning - first, now that Silverjet has three aircraft and two destinations (yes, for the female population of Dubai, he flies there too) the odds of him being on your flight are much diminished.

And second, even I realise that while it might be an entertaining idea, selecting goods or services based on the chief executive's looks is not the most sensible course of action for a woman running a business. There are, after all, places I need to go other than New York and Dubai.

However, choosing a carrier because it has its own terminal - and this for a mere three departures a day - makes perfect sense, and just in case I needed reminding, I departed from Heathrow just after Christmas to spend New Year in the Caribbean. This was a lot less glamorous than it sounds and Heathrow, to be fair, was the least of the problems. Virgin Atlantic's exhortation to cut down on time spent at the airport by checking-in online proved impossible three times over - remotely on my computer (the website just refused, even after half an hour on the phone to Virgin); at the airport automatic check-in kiosk ("Sorry, we cannot print at the moment"); and then even when a helpful assistant took me off to her terminal, which promptly jammed.

So we stood in line for an hour for the so-called "bag drop" which wasn't functioning as a bag drop at all, but as an old-fashioned check-in.

And with Lawrence Hunt's best interests at heart, I can see the hazards of any individual being associated so strongly with a brand. By the time Mr M's in-seat entertainment had failed to function in spite of repeated re-setting by the cabin crew, any appearance by Sir Richard Branson would have resulted in my husband being arrested for assault.

We (and that included me) flew to Barbados in economy. As regular readers will know, I firmly believe that children should not fly business class until they can pay for it themselves, and that the under-12s should be banned from the first-class cabin. But even allowing for those strictures, taking a family of five to the Caribbean in peak season is still prohibitively expensive. And thanks to the malfunctioning of the Virgin check-in system we were seated all over the place. Cost Centre #1 ended up in a window seat far away from me, next to a mother/daughter combo that, shall we say, did not strike me as the likeliest dinner companions for him.

I occasionally cast a glance in his direction during the flight and, to my concern, saw him flashing his £2,500 of orthodontistry at them, a tactic guaranteed to melt the heart of even the most hard-bitten female.

When I met him later in the queue for the loo, I urged caution - you have to be careful who you smile at in economy. Look at me. I met his father while travelling at the back of the plane. Nineteen years of marriage and three cost centres later, and here I am standing in The World of Golf on East 47th Street asking if they stock Titleist NXT Tour balls.

THE MONSTROUS REGIMENTS

Jan 19, 2008

Women can be quite terrifying in large numbers. I am sure that men can be as well, but I am always slightly intimidated by large groups of women, especially when organised into fighting units.

I have written before about my views on women-only networks and organisations. I believe in women supporting each other in this male-dominated world, and were I a US citizen I would be voting for Hillary for that reason alone, but does such support need to be a formal arrangement?

Many large companies have women's networks and I am always suspicious that the reason they are encouraged and supported (usually by a male-dominated management) is that they might provide some protection for those companies against the day they receive a lawsuit alleging sex discrimination. Many of these companies are quoted and I am not sure this is a good use of shareholders' money. Why not just pay higher premiums to insure against lawsuits? Women's networks seem a bit too PC for my liking - right up there with organic vegetables and Pilates.

This is perhaps a rather jaundiced view, but it is one that I ventured at the 2007 Women's Forum in Deauville last October. Here were 1,000 participants (mostly women, and so fairly terrifying) debating the social and economic issues of the day. It was like a female-led version of the World Economic Forum, only by the sea in France rather than up a mountain in Switzerland.

Of course I do believe that women need support - it remains harder for a woman to get started and succeed in her career, whether as an employee or an entrepreneur, than for a man. But do we need to institutionalise that support? I run, in effect, a network, in that I have a great many female friends and acquaintances who hold senior positions and run businesses, and I introduce them to each other and encourage them to support each other. That is exactly what men do, after all.

Having said all that, I am a grudging admirer of some organisations, such as Vital Voices, the Washington DC-based not-for-profit body that grandly declares that it "empowers" women. What it actually does is to invest in women around the world, mainly in places a bit further away and a bit more under-resourced than the ones my girlfriends inhabit. Typically, the women that Vital Voices supports are pioneers in economic, political and social advancement in their countries, and it is this type of support that I applaud.

Vital Voices does have a couple of UK-based women on its board, including the redoubtable life peer Mary Goudie.

I have long been a fan, not merely of Goudie, but of her business card, which she had printed the first time she had to work with civil servants. On the front it gives her contact details and proclaims her as a member of the House of Lords. The reverse bears the following instruction: "Those who say it cannot be done ... should not interrupt those who are doing it." A marvellous sentiment.

Vital Voices was represented at the Women's Forum in Deauville, as were the 200 or so women who participate in the Rallye Aicha des Gazelles, the women-only desert navigation rally held each year in Morocco. As a speaker at the forum, I was met at the Gare du Nord and driven to Deauville by one of them, a very glamorous woman. Another one, this time a lady just retired from a lifetime working at Renault, drove me back a day later. Why did they give up valuable time to come and staff the car service at the Women's Forum? I was told that not only did they get to attend the sessions for free, but they also made useful contacts with people who subsequently became sponsors.

If sponsorship is a little beyond your means or inclination, I commend to you, female or male, the 2008 calendar produced by the Gazelles. Not only is it in a good cause (to raise money to buy bicycles for Moroccan schoolchildren), but it costs only €20, from www.rallyeaichadesgazelles.com. Best of all, it is gloriously un-PC - Pirelli, eat your heart out. And it won't terrify anyone.

Cold comforts

Jan 26, 2008

A group of people in a small Swiss ski resort at 1,500m will this weekend debate the pressing issues of the world. Before packing my snow boots, I considered how I was likely to contribute to the debate on world trends.

One of the big discussions is likely to be about the rising price of food. As large parts of the developing world become more affluent and start eating meat, and as demand for biofuels continues to grow, the prices of agricultural produce will rise and food will become more expensive. I considered my own experience of this. If the entire Moneypenny clan was at home all the time, and the cost centres were not outsourced to boarding school, I estimate that we would spend 10 per cent of our monthly net income on food - and that includes eating out. This means that I am likely to be price-insensitive to food, as it remains such a relatively small part of my total expenditure. Against the school fees, it is almost an insignificant sum. And of course, that 10 per cent does not include the cost of preparing the meals. The price of energy is rising as well, and so also will the running costs of an Aga fired by natural gas and an electric microwave (my sole cooking appliances).

And even if I were not price-insensitive to food, what would be my benchmarks anyway? Years ago, when I had a job following the fortunes of Britain's supermarkets, I learned that most people who regularly shop for food are able to carry about 10 Known Value Items in their head - things they buy regularly and whose prices they are keenly aware of. If these prices go up, they notice. My only KVI, I now realise, is a kilo of back bacon, which is £5 in my local butcher and considerably more in the supermarket.

No, my real interest in this subject concerns the office. In our company, we feed everyone (or offer to) while they are at work. The cost of providing daytime food for a workforce smaller than a couple of dozen people in west London is nowhere near 10 per cent of the net income of the company. It can also be set against corporation tax in the UK, as long as you offer the same benefit to all staff. So no directors' dining room, and no special shelf in the fridge for select employees.

Our food comes via a weekly delivery from a supermarket. And while the cost of food has certainly been going up, so too has the cost of having the supermarket deliver it. When we started ordering from the supermarket on the internet, this was free, but that came to an end long ago.

Inspecting the fridge to review the changing eating habits of my team - hardly a proxy for the world population, I admit - I have noticed an increasing quantity of what I would call luxury goods. This is of course a staff-retention strategy. Our low employee turnover does not indicate a lack of interest among our rivals in poaching our staff, and they are all regularly approached by other employers. One of my team told me that she had rebuffed one recent advance by explaining that we had smoked salmon in the fridge and that she thought it unlikely that this benefit would be available if she moved.

One of the downsides of employing large numbers of women, as we do, especially ones in their twenties and thirties, is that they seem either to be on a diet or pregnant. This may be an office (rather than a world) trend, but I am convinced that this is why we never have any decent butter. Instead, we have *butter* that seems to me more chemicals and air than dairy produce, and that tastes disgusting.

To alter the butter policy of the office might be a little draconian, and eating this stuff is probably good for me anyway. But I confess that I long for office birthdays. Whenever one comes around, the diets go out of the window and one of our team who is a very talented cake-maker turns up with one of her delicious creations. She ices it in the office, and occasionally brings in real butter for this purpose.

I notice that she hides it at the back of the fridge (no doubt hoping it will still be there for the next cake) but I have no hesitation in using it for the next baked potato or piece of toast that I am compelled to consume while working late at my desk.

The rising price of dairy produce is indeed a world trend, and no doubt will be mentioned in the snow at Davos.

I only hope that we eventually buy enough proper butter for it to become noticeable to me.